ON CONAN DOYLE

WRITERS ON WRITERS

MICHAEL DIRDA ▣ **ON CONAN DOYLE**

or, The Whole Art

of Storytelling

PRINCETON UNIVERSITY PRESS

Princeton and Oxford

Requests for permission to reproduce material from this work
should be sent to Permissions, Princeton University Press

Published by Princeton University Press, 41 William Street,
Princeton, New Jersey 08540
In the United Kingdom: Princeton University Press, 6 Oxford
Street, Woodstock, Oxfordshire OX20 1TW

press.princeton.edu

Jacket illustration: *Sir Arthur Conan Doyle Reading at His Home*,
ca.1912; photograph © E. O. Hoppé/Corbis

Library of Congress Cataloging-in-Publication Data
Dirda, Michael.
   On Conan Doyle, or, The whole art of storytelling / Michael
Dirda.
        p. cm. — (Writers on writers)
   Includes bibliographical references.
   ISBN 978-0-691-15135-9 (hardcover : alk. paper)   1. Doyle,
Arthur Conan, Sir, 1859–1930—Criticism and interpretation.
I. Title.   II. Title: On Conan Doyle.   III. Title: Whole art of
storytelling.
   PR4624.D57 2011
   823'.8—dc23

                                        2011020674

British Library Cataloging-in-Publication Data is available

This book has been composed in Minion Pro with Myriad Pro
Printed on acid-free paper. ∞
Printed in the United States of America

10 9 8 7 6 5 4 3 2 1

For The Baker Street Irregulars

▨ CONTENTS

"You Know My Methods, Watson"

◻ Graham Greene famously observed that only in childhood do books have any deep influence on our lives. "In later life, we admire, we are entertained, we may modify some views we already hold, but we are more likely to find in books merely a confirmation of what is in our minds already." But when we are young, "all books are books of divination, telling us about the future, and like the fortune-teller who sees a long journey in the cards or death by water they influence the future."

Had he not loved the swashbucklers of Stanley J. Weyman (*Under the Red Robe*) and Marjorie Bowen (*The Viper of Milan*), would Greene have written *This Gun for Hire* and *The Third Man*? How many adults first learned about moral complexity from the final chapter of Beverly Cleary's *Henry Huggins,* when the dog Ribsy must choose between two equally kind masters? Who, at any age, can read unmoved the last pages of *Tarzan of the Apes* when the rightful Lord Greystoke, deliberating sacrificing his own hope for happiness, quietly says, "My mother was an ape . . . I never knew who my father was." In our hearts, we measure all the "better" and "greater" books of adulthood against such touchstones—and in later years we often return to the originals for comfort and renewal. That arch-sophisticate Noel Coward passed his final days rereading *Five Children and It, The Story of the Treasure Seekers,* and the other children's classics of E. Nesbit.

On Conan Doyle, or, The Whole Art of Storytelling is a book about the pleasures of reading, a celebration of plot and atmosphere, adventure and romance, and an invitation to go beyond the Sherlock Holmes stories to explore a remarkable body of writing. Its slightly old-fashioned subtitle recalls the sleuth of Baker Street's long planned, but apparently never written, masterwork: *The Whole Art of Detection.* Structured as a kind of reader's memoir, *On Conan Doyle* begins with my own youthful discovery of *The Hound of the Baskervilles*, then looks at the Professor Challenger adventures and the great tales of terror and the supernatural. There's a chapter on Conan Doyle's nonfiction, concentrating on his memoirs, personal essays, and fiercely polemical journalism, and another on his "neglected" fiction, touching on such books as the medieval swashbuckler *The White Company* and the social novels *Beyond the City, The Stark Munro Letters, A Duet with an Occasional Chorus,* and *The Tragedy of the "Korosko."* Since every Sherlock Holmes fan has heard of that mysterious literary society, The Baker Street Irregulars, *On Conan Doyle* also provides an insider's account of its curiously romantic activities and traditions, as well as an example of what Irregulars call "the grand game." I then conclude with some final reflections on the afterlife of Sherlock Holmes and Dr. Watson.

A last point: In general, I reveal as little as possible about the action or plots of Conan Doyle's various stories and novels. I tell enough to bolster an argument or illustrate some aspect of style, but no more. *On Conan Doyle* aims, above all, to enhance, not detract from, the reader's pleasure in the wonderful fiction and nonfiction to which we now turn.

■ ON CONAN DOYLE

"A Hound It Was"

Sometime in the mid-1990s I was lucky enough to interview Robert Madle, a dealer in science fiction and fantasy pulp magazines, as well as a member of First Fandom, the now much-diminished group—never large—of those pimply teens who attended the inaugural 1939 World Science Fiction Convention.

"Every so often," Madle told me, "I'll get a call from somebody looking for, say, *Astounding* from 1934 to 1937, and I immediately know this is a guy in his seventies hoping to relive his youth, who wants to reread the stories of his childhood." When young, these doctors, lawyers, and businessmen had studied with longing the corner drugstore racks gaudy with issues of *Weird Tales*, *Black Mask*, *The Shadow*, and *Thrilling Wonder Stories*. Now retired, these old men—and a few women—yearned to feel again some flicker of youth's incomparable freshness when every magazine and cheap paperback proffered a vision of how exciting life was going to be. And never quite is.

Still, a few books retain more of their magic than others.

The Hound of the Baskervilles (1902), by Arthur Conan Doyle, was the first "grown-up" book I ever read—and it changed my life. Back in the late 1950s my fifth-grade class belonged to an elementary school book club. Each month our teacher would pass out a four-page newsletter describing several dozen paperbacks available for purchase. I remember buying Jim Kjelgaard's *Big Red* and a thriller called *Treasure at First Base*, as well as Geoffrey Household's *Mystery of the Spanish Cave*. (Years later, I would race through Household's famous *Rogue Male*, about the English hunter who tries to assassinate Hitler and who instead finds himself relentlessly tracked and pursued.) Lying on my bed at home, I lingered for hours over these newsprint catalogs, carefully making my final selections.

I had to. Each month my mother would allow me to purchase no more than four of the twenty-five- and thirty-five-cent paperbacks. Not even constant wheedling and abject supplication could shake her resolve. "What do you think we are, made of money? What's wrong with the library?"

After Mr. Jackson sent in the class's order, several weeks would pass and I would almost, but not quite, forget which books I had ordered. Then in the middle of some dull afternoon, probably given over to the arcane mysteries of addition and subtraction, a teacher's aide would open the classroom door and silently drop off a big, heavily taped parcel. Whispers would ripple up and down the rows and everyone would grow restive, hoping that the goodies would be distributed that very minute. Sometimes we would be made to wait an entire day, especially if the package had been delivered close to the three o'clock bell when school let out.

Romantic poets regularly sigh over their childhood memories of splendor in the grass, of glory in the flower. But what are daisies and rainbows compared to four sleek and shiny paperbacks? After more than thirty years as a literary journalist, I have seen and reviewed new books aplenty. Ah, but then, then, at my wooden school desk, etched with generations of student initials, I would methodically appraise each volume's artwork, read and reread its back cover, carefully investigate the delicate line of glue at the top edge of the perfect-bound spines. Afterwards, I would glance around, sometimes with barely suppressed envy, to survey the gleaming treasures on the desks nearby. Certainly no rare first editions have ever been so carefully handled and cherished as those apparently ordinary book-club paperbacks.

To this day I can more or less recall the news-letter's capsule summary that compelled me to buy *The Hound of the Baskervilles*—as if that ominous title alone weren't enough! Beneath a small reproduction of the paperback's cover—depicting a shadowy Something with fiery eyes crouching on a moonlit crag—blazed the thrilling words: "What was it that emerged from the moor at night to spread terror and violent death?" What else, of course, but a monstrous hound from the bowels of Hell? When I opened my very own copy of the book, the beast was further described on the inside display page:

A hound it was, an enormous coal-black hound, but not such a hound as mortal eyes have ever seen. Fire burst from its open mouth, its eyes glowed with a smoldering glare, its muzzle and hackles and dewlap were outlined in flickering flame. Never in the delirious dream of a disordered brain could anything more savage, more appalling, more hellish, be conceived than that dark form and savage face which broke upon us out of the wall of fog.

Eager as I was to start immediately on this almost irresistible treat, I staunchly determined to put off reading the book until I could do so under just the right conditions. At the very least, I required a dark and stormy night, and the utter absence of distracting sisters and parents. Finally, there came a Saturday in early November when my mother and father announced that they would be visiting relatives that evening—and "the girls" would be going along. Yes, I might stay at home alone to read. The afternoon soon grew a dull metallic gray, threatening rain.

With a dollar clutched in my fist, I pedaled my red Roadmaster bike to Whalen's drugstore, where I quickly picked out two or three candy bars, a box of Cracker Jack, and a cold bottle of Orange Crush. After my family had driven off in our new 1958 Ford, I dragged a blanket from my bed, spread it on the reclining chair next to the living room's brass floor lamp, carefully arranged my provisions near to hand, turned off all the other lights in the house, and crawled expectantly under the covers with my paperback of *The Hound*—just as the heavens began to boom with thunder and the rain to thump against the curtained windows.

In the louring darkness I turned page after page, more than a little scared, gradually learning the origin of the dreaded curse of the Baskervilles. At the end of the book's second chapter, you may recall, the tension escalates unbearably. Holmes and Watson have just been told how Sir Charles Baskerville has been found dead, apparently running *away* from the safety of his own house. Their informant Dr. Mortimer pauses, then adds, hesitantly, that near the body he had spotted footprints on the damp ground. A man's or a woman's? eagerly inquires the great detective, to which question he receives the most thrilling answer in all of twentieth-century literature: "Mr. Holmes, they were the footprints of a gigantic hound!" I shivered with fearful pleasure, scrunched further down under my thick blanket, and took another bite of my Baby Ruth candy bar, as happy as I will ever be.

To my surprise, I would later discover that my first meeting with Mr. Sherlock Holmes and Dr. John H. Watson was hardly distinctive, let alone unique. Conan Doyle's own daughter Jean used to read her father's stories by flashlight in bed. One of the two cousins—probably Frederic Dannay rather than Manfred Lee—who together concocted the Ellery Queen mysteries relates his own version of my story. Suffering from an earache, he was lying in bed when an aunt unexpectedly came to visit and brought along a book from the public library:

It was *The Adventures of Sherlock Holmes*. I opened the book with no realization that I stood, or rather sat, on the brink of my fate. I had no inkling, no premonition, that in another minute my life's work, such as it is, would be born.

My first glance was disheartening. I saw the frontispiece of the Harper edition—a picture of a rather innocuous man in dress coat and striped trousers holding the arm of a young woman in a bridal gown. A love story, I said to myself, for surely this unattractive couple were in a church about to be married. . . . Only an unknown and unknowable sixth sense prompted me to turn to the table of contents and then the world brightened. The first story, "A Scandal in Bohemia," seemed to hold little red-blooded promise, but the next story was, and always will be, a milestone. A strange rushing thrill challenged the pain in my ear. "The Red-Headed League"! What a combination of simple words to skewer themselves into the brain of a hungry boy! I glanced down quickly, "The Man with the Twisted Lip," "The Adventure of the Speckled Band" and I was lost! Ecstatically, everlastingly lost!

I finished *The Adventures* that night. . . . As I closed the book, I knew that I had read one of the greatest books ever written. And today I realize with amazement how true and tempered was my twelve-year-old critical sense. For in the mature smugness of my present literary judgment, I still feel unalterably that *The Adventures* is one of the world's masterworks.

As indeed it is.

In my own case, the romance of that Dartmoor hellhound would lead me to Conan Doyle's other books, to the work of his peers and followers, and eventually to the recognition that "the observance of trifles," as Holmes called his method, lay at the heart of literary criticism. Eventually, too, I would discover a group of friends, from the most varied backgrounds, who shared a passion for what have been called the Sacred Writings: the almost legendary Baker Street Irregulars. Yet little did I then suspect—as the narrators in old-time mysteries are wont to say—that forty years after that rainy night in Lorain, Ohio, I would be proposing a toast to the Hound at a banquet in honor of the one-hundredth anniversary of Arthur Conan Doyle's most thrilling novel. But I get ahead of myself.

"Elementary"

Sir Arthur Ignatius Conan Doyle (1859–1930) wasn't knighted in 1902 for creating Sherlock Holmes, though many readers feel he should have been. The literary journalist Christopher Morley, founder of The Baker Street Irregulars, declared that he actually should have been sainted. In fact, Arthur Conan Doyle only reluctantly added Sir to his name—for his services and writings during the Boer Wars—because his beloved mother talked him into it. On his books he austerely remained A. Conan Doyle "without," as he said, "any trimmings." Such modesty is characteristic of this altogether remarkable man, one who gave his own stolid John Bull appearance, down to the military mustache, not to his Great Detective but to the loyal Dr. Watson.

Appropriately, Conan Doyle once named "unaffectedness" as his own favorite virtue, then listed "'manliness' as his favorite virtue in another man; 'work' as his favorite occupation; 'time well filled' as his ideal of happiness; 'men who do their duty' as his favorite heroes in real life; and 'affectation and conceit' as his pet aversions." It should thus come as no surprise that Conan Doyle's books are all fairly transparent endorsements of the chivalric ideals of honor, duty, courage, and greatness of heart.

In Javier Maria's charming volume of essays called *Written Lives*, the Spanish novelist retells a well-known story about the writer and his family. Sir Arthur was traveling by train through South Africa and "one of his grown-up sons commented on the ugliness of a woman who happened to walk down the corridor. He had barely had time to finish this sentence when he received a slap and saw, very close to his, the flushed face of his old father, who said very mildly: 'Just remember that no woman is ugly.'" While no man is on oath for lapidary inscriptions, nearly every student of Conan Doyle agrees that as man, writer, and citizen he strove to live up to the knightly words etched on his tombstone: "Steel true, blade straight."

Arthur Conan Doyle was born and brought up in Edinburgh, Scotland, the third child and elder son of a large Irish family. Art ran in the Doyle blood, for his grandfather John, uncle Richard, and father Charles were all noted Victorian illustrators. But Conan Doyle's immediate family was hardly rich and eventually quite poor due to his father's alcoholism and general fecklessness. (Eventually Charles Doyle was committed to a mental asylum, though arguments persist over whether this was needed or simply convenient.) By his mother's scrimping, young Arthur was nonetheless educated at the prestigious Jesuit school, Stonyhurst College, and eventually attended Edinburgh University, where he trained to become a doctor.

By his early twenties, A. Conan Doyle had begun to publish short stories—many of them tales of mystery and the uncanny—and for several years balanced an averagely successful medical practice with part-time authorship. In 1887, the novella-length *A Study in Scarlet* introduced Sherlock Holmes to the world, though no special acclaim followed. Instead the young writer initially gained attention as a historical novelist, first with *Micah Clarke* (1889), set in the seventeenth century during the Monmouth Rebellion, and then with *The White Company* (1891). The latter—about a medieval cohort of English archers—was largely read as a thrilling work of escapism, much to the annoyance of its author, who insisted that it was intended to portray and instill all the most noble British values.

A second Sherlock Holmes novel, *The Sign of the Four*, appeared in 1889; but only in 1891, when short stories about the consulting detective

began to be serialized in the *Strand Magazine*—
they were later collected as *The Adventures of
Sherlock Holmes* (1892)—did Baker Street mania
finally sweep the public. By then Conan Doyle
had launched himself as a full-time professional
writer. Astonishingly, as early as 1891 he had already written to his mother that he was thinking
of "slaying" Holmes because producing mysteries for the detective to solve kept him from working on "better things." In 1893 Conan Doyle duly
brought out "The Final Problem," which became
the last story in *The Memoirs of Sherlock Holmes*
(1893). In its pages the great detective and his
archenemy Professor James Moriarty meet on a
mountain pass in Switzerland for "the final discussion of those questions which lie between
us." Grappling together, they eventually plum-
met to their deaths in the swirling waters of the
Reichenbach Falls. The whole world mourned.

During the subsequent decade Conan Doyle
published a novel or work of nonfiction nearly
every year, as well as a series of rousing short stories about a Napoleonic hussar named Etienne
Gerard. In 1902, however, he finally relented and
brought back Holmes in the phenomenally successful *Hound of the Baskervilles,* insisting that
the novel represented a pre-Reichenbach adven-

ture. By this time Holmes's creator was not just one of the highest paid authors in the world, but also very much a public intellectual. Conan Doyle regularly lent his name and pen to causes in which he believed: divorce law reform, the plight of abused Africans in the Congo, miscarriages of criminal justice, the need for military preparedness, and, eventually, Spiritualism.

Though he might portray his detective as prey to moodiness and an almost decadent languor, the outgoing and athletic Conan Doyle more closely resembled a hearty than an aesthete. While young and poor he worked for several months on an Arctic whaler, and was reportedly offered the chance to become its harpooner. In his middle years, he kept active by hiking, bicycling, riding, golfing, shooting, hunting, and taking part in games of all sorts. He played competitive billiards, enjoyed boxing, and skied regularly, being one of the first to bring the Scandinavian sport to Switzerland. For many years Conan Doyle even belonged to a rather literary cricket team called the Allahakbarries, its name punningly combining the Arabic formula praising God with a nod to the team's captain J. M. Barrie (creator of Peter Pan). Conan Doyle was actually good enough as a cricketeer to face England's legendary W. G. Grace, widely regarded as the greatest player in the history of the game.

To the world, however, all that mattered were the Sherlock Holmes stories, and finally, in 1903, new adventures of the great detective began to be serialized in the *Strand Magazine*. Holmes, it turned out, had never really been dead: For three years, using the name Sigerson, he had been lying low in Tibet and undertaking arcane chemical research in Europe. While these post-Reichenbach stories, collected as *The Return of Sherlock Holmes* (1905), include some of the detective's most notable achievements ("The Priory School," "The Dancing Men" "The Second Stain"), many readers felt that after his so-called "great hiatus" Holmes wasn't quite the man he used to be.

In 1907, following the death of his first wife Louise from tuberculosis, Arthur Conan Doyle married Jean Leckie, with whom he had been in love for a decade. That same year he gathered his reflections on reading, writing, and his favorite books into a volume titled, somewhat sentimentally but honestly, *Through the Magic Door*. With 1912's *The Lost World* Conan Doyle introduced his second most famous character, the blustery Professor George Edward Challenger, who guides an expedition deep into the South American jungle to a plateau where dinosaurs still roam the earth. It was followed a year later by a second Challenger adventure, *The Poison Belt* (1913), in which a cosmic gas threatens to kill nearly every living creature on earth.

During the First World War Conan Doyle worked on a six-volume history of the British campaign in Europe. He also began to acknowledge publicly the truth of Spiritualism and to proclaim that through séances one could contact loved ones on the Other Side. He quickly transformed himself, with his usual energy, into an active Spiritualist crusader, traveling to Europe, North America, South Africa, and even Australia, often with his family in tow. Meanwhile, the final volumes devoted to Sherlock Holmes's recorded cases—*The Valley of Fear* (1915), *His Last Bow* (1917), and, especially, *The Case-Book of Sherlock Holmes* (1927)—addressed a greater range of human suffering, as well as the brutality, sexualization, and violence of the modern world. The autobiographical *Memories and Adventures* first appeared in 1924 and was later revised, just before the author's death, to cover more fully his later Spiritualist activities.

Sir Arthur Conan Doyle died of a heart attack in 1930 at the age of 71. Over the course of a fifty-year writing career he published 21 novels and more than 150 short stories, as well as hundreds of letters to the press, a great deal of nonfiction, and three volumes of poetry. Along the way, he created many striking characters, including two of such vitality that generations of readers have instinctively believed, or wanted to believe, that they were as real as you or I: the consulting detective Mr. Sherlock Holmes and his chronicler and friend Dr. John H. Watson.

"A Most Dark and Sinister Business"

▣ *The Hound of the Baskervilles* left its teeth marks in me and seriously aroused my then still slumbering passion for reading. I was no longer the same ten-year-old when I reached its final pages: "'I said it in London, Watson, and I say it again now, that never yet have we helped to hunt down a more dangerous man than he who is lying yonder'—he swept his long arm toward the huge mottled expanse of green-splotched bog which stretched away until it merged into the russet slopes of the moor." I closed the book with a pang of loss.

My initial, and surprisingly sensible, impulse was to head immediately for my local branch library, located a short bike ride away in Lorain Plaza Shopping Center. (It's a sad reflection of our misplaced civic priorities that that neighborhood cultural center was shuttered during a lean economy and never reopened, its space being taken over by, successively, a Radio Shack outlet, a pizza joint, and a cell phone store.) Only a single book by A. Conan Doyle was listed in the card catalog, but it was the right one: the venerable Doubleday edition of *The Complete Sherlock Holmes*. This time I started with *A Study in Scarlet*, in which John H. Watson, wounded at the battle of Maiwand, is discharged from the army, returns to London, and there learns of a rather unusual chap looking for someone to share the cost of lodgings.

"Dr. Watson, Mr. Sherlock Holmes," said Stamford, introducing us.

"How are you?" he said cordially, gripping my hand with a strength for which I should hardly have given him credit. "You have been in Afghanistan, I perceive."

"How on earth did you know that?" I asked in astonishment.

"Never mind," said he, chuckling to himself. . . .

Watson's astonished question—"How on earth did you know that?"—already hints at one of the major themes, and much of the perennial fascination, of the Sherlock Holmes stories. We lesser mortals may see, but the great detective alone observes, reasons, and correctly deduces. "It is my business to know things," he declares in "The Blanched Soldier." "That is my trade."

At some point during the two-week check-out period in which *The Complete Sherlock Holmes* was mine alone, I went back and read Christopher Morley's introduction, perhaps the most revered of all Sherlockian essays. Here this popular novelist and journalist of the 1930s and '40s recalls racing home at night from the Enoch Pratt Free Library in Baltimore, pausing for a moment under each streetlight to scan just one more paragraph of some fresh Conan Doyle volume. For Morley, as for me and so many others, the assembled Sherlock Holmes stories were far more than a large book with small type: They were nothing less than "an encyclopedia of romance," the "triumphant illustration of art's supremacy over life."

According to Herbert Greenhough Smith, the longtime editor of the *Strand Magazine*, Arthur Conan Doyle was simply "the greatest natural-born storyteller of the age." Today I might argue that this honor should rightfully be shared with Rudyard Kipling, but Conan Doyle certainly stands unrivaled for crisp narrative economy. He achieves powerful and often highly poetic effects through a first-person prose that is plain, direct, frequently epigrammatic, and mysteriously ingratiating. This last and most important attribute Vladimir Nabokov once called *shamanstvo*—the enchanter-quality. Start a story by Conan Doyle and you cannot stop reading, whether you are ten or sixty. Just listen for instance to the opening paragraph of "A Scandal in Bohemia":

To Sherlock Holmes she is always *the* woman. I have seldom heard him mention her under any other name. In his eyes she eclipses and predominates the whole of her sex. It was not that he felt any emotion akin to love for Irene Adler. All emotions, and that one particularly, were abhorrent to his cold, precise but admirably balanced mind. He was, I take it, the most perfect reasoning and observing machine that the world has seen, but as a lover he would have placed himself in a false position. He never spoke of the softer passions, save with a gibe and a sneer. They were admirable things for the observer—excellent for drawing the veil from men's motives and actions. But for the trained reasoner to admit such intrusions into his own delicate and finely adjusted temperament was to introduce a distracting factor which might throw a doubt upon all his mental results. Grit in a sensitive instrument, or a crack in one of his own high-power lenses, would not be more disturbing than a strong emotion in a nature such as his. And yet there was but one woman to him, and that woman was the late Irene Adler, of dubious and questionable memory.

Despite years of teacherly reproof, I have never been able to stop moving my lips while reading. As a result, murmuring the above sentences to myself for the nth time even now produces a series of little bursts of what I must call verbal happiness, an almost child-like joy over Watson's succession of flourishes and turns of phrase. This, in truth, is why one reads: for delight, for excitement. The classicist A. E. Housman confessed that he could recognize great poetry by a certain tingle at the back of his neck, even as Roland Barthes would later expatiate about the almost sexual "pleasure of the text."

Have italics ever been so brilliantly employed as in the phrase "*the* woman"? A sentence like "He never spoke of the softer passions, save with a gibe and a sneer" generates its own verbal music through the repetition of the *s* sounds and the unexpected rightness of the old-fashioned "save" instead of the usual "except." Not least, Watson ends with the sudden electrical charge of that exquisitely tantalizing final phrase, "of dubious and questionable memory." For, of course, Irene Adler was just a Victorian adventuress, the kept woman of a king. And yet . . . .

From the beginning of his career, like any *chevalier sans peur et sans reproche*, Holmes makes clear his hatred for baseness and cruelty, with a special disdain reserved for aristocratic callousness and the plutocrat's casual abuse of privilege. In this instance, the detective conceals neither his admiration for the indomitable woman who actually outsmarts him nor his utter contempt for the smug King of Bohemia. "Is it not a pity that she was not on my level?" says the king, to which Holmes coldly replies, "From what I have seen of the lady, she seems, indeed, to be on a very different level to your Majesty."

The investigation of crime inevitably spills over into considerations of motive and justification, punishment and mercy. The Sherlock Holmes stories are never just murder mysteries, they are moral fictions. Down Baker Street and every mean byway of London a man boldly goes who is neither tarnished nor afraid, though he wears an Inverness cape rather than Philip Marlowe's trench coat. Holmes, for all his eccentricities and neurotic tics, will never bow to cant, will always do what he believes to be right, and will faithfully ride to the rescue of the suffering and desperate. As he once said, "In over a thousand cases I am not aware that I have ever used my powers upon the wrong side." Some stories, however, address matters that must have shocked many early readers. Consider, for instance, "The Yellow Face," which ultimately turns on a woman's previous marriage. At its climax, Mrs. Grant Munro touches a spring on the locket she always wears:

> There was a portrait within of a man, strikingly handsome and intelligent, but bearing unmistakable signs upon his features of his African descent.
>
> "That is John Hebron, of Atlanta," said the lady, "and a nobler man never walked the earth. I cut myself off from my race in order to

wed him, but never once while he lived did I for one instant regret it."

"The Yellow Face," which was published in 1893, concludes with Grant Munro opening his arms to his wife's long concealed and very dark-skinned little girl: "I am not a very good man, Effie, but I think that I am a better one than you have given me credit for being."

In the course of our lives, we naturally read Watson's tales of Holmes's exploits for myriad reasons: When young, for the expertly paced and thrilling plots; when older, to return to cozy, gaslit 1895 when all seemed right with the world, or at least when the world itself still seemed rightable. In our later years, we relish the vignettes of Baker Street domesticity, smile at the cross-talk between detective and doctor, and wait eagerly for those particular Holmesian idioms that so enchant. "It is perhaps less suggestive than it might have been," remarks the detective in "The Blue Carbuncle"—that "Christmas story without slush," as Christopher Morley once called it—as he examines an old hat for what it reveals of its owner:

and yet there are a few inferences which are very distinct, and a few others which represent at least a strong balance of probability. That the man was highly intellectual is of course obvious upon the face of it, and also that he was fairly well-to-do within the last three years, although he has now fallen upon evil days. He had foresight, but has less now than formerly, pointing to a moral retrogression, which, when taken with the decline of his fortunes, seems to indicate some evil influence, probably drink, at work upon him. This may account also for the obvious fact that his wife has ceased to love him.

"That his wife has ceased to love him." Holmes never could resist his little *coups de théâtre.* "By a man's fingernails, by his coat-sleeve, by his boots, by his trouser-knees, by the callosities of his forefinger and thumb, by his expression, by his shirt-cuffs—by each of these things a man's calling is plainly revealed." Pipes, hats, walking sticks, cigarette cases, polished coffee pots, bootlaces—all these surrender breathtaking insights. "You mentioned your name," says the detective in "The Norwood Builder," "as if I should recognize it, but I assure you that, beyond the obvious facts that you are a bachelor, a solicitor, a Freemason, and an asthmatic, I know nothing whatever about you." Conan Doyle himself learned the art of deduction from his medical school training. After all, an overwrought client visiting 221B Baker Street resembles nothing so much as a desperate patient seeking answers and relief from a medical specialist. In most of his operations, Holmes acts first as the probing diagnostician and later as the surgeon who confronts the cancer and plies the knife.

As it happens, when Robert Louis Stevenson read the early adventures of Sherlock Holmes, he wrote to their author from Samoa asking if the detective were modeled on his "old friend Joe Bell." Conan Doyle readily admitted that this noted Edinburgh professor of surgery was his inspiration. Joseph Bell's percipience, and theatricality, obviously approached a Sherlockian brilliance. "Ah," Bell might announce to his students after quickly glancing at a new patient, "you are a soldier, and a non-commissioned officer at that. You have served in Bermuda. Now how do I know that, gentlemen? Because he came into the room without even taking his hat off, as he would go into an orderly room. He was a soldier. A slight, authoritative air, combined with his age, shows that he was a non-commissioned officer. A rash on his forehead tells me he was in Bermuda and subject to a certain rash only known there." Neatly enough, Bell's own mentor was an equally famous surgeon with the name Dr. Watson, albeit Dr. Patrick Heron Watson.

As a boy, I obviously knew nothing of Joseph Bell and little more of Arthur Conan Doyle. What mattered was simply that the Sherlock Holmes stories were even better than Tarzan movies and Green Lantern comics. Let me add that this was no mean feat. Nonetheless, the dark day inevitably dawned when I had read everything that Dr. Watson had recorded about his friend. What could I turn to next? Would I ever again discover any stories even half so good? And how would I ever find them? My working-class parents didn't read books, no self-respecting kid would ask a teacher for advice, and the public library's adult shelves were still off-limits.

Yet as Hamlet—that most Sherlockian of Shakespeare's characters—once observed, there's a divinity that shapes our ends, rough-hew them how we will. One Saturday afternoon at children's catechism class I picked up that week's *Junior Catholic Messenger* and noticed that the issue was headlined "The Blue Cross." No doubt, I presumed with pubescent cynicism, the saccharine account of some miracle in an obscure province of Italy or central Mexico. However, our parish priest was running late, so I started to read in the dim half-light of St. Vitus Church, first casually, then with mounting excitement. "Flambeau was in England!" A Gallic criminal mastermind of immense and showy cleverness, Flambeau, for all his gifts, was nonetheless eventually thwarted by a mousy little priest named Father Brown. That was astonishing in itself, but far more important than G. K. Chesterton's mixture of mystery and Mystery was his almost lip-smacking narrative gusto.

After I finished "The Blue Cross," I soon hied my way back to the branch library in Lorain Plaza for a copy of *The Father Brown Omnibus*. As with the Sherlock Holmes stories, I greedily gobbled them down in just a few weeks, never being what you would call moderate in my passions. To this day those Father Brown titles deliver cozy shivers: "The Hammer of God," "The Sins of Prince Saradine," "The Invisible Man," "The Oracle of the Dog." Each story chronicled a crime utterly beyond human ken and often smelling of black magic. Yet Father Brown revealed, again and again, that mind alone—supported by a deep understanding of and sympathy with fallen human nature—could solve any riddle.

Notwithstanding my high regard for the shrewd cleric, I couldn't forswear my initial admiration for the daring criminal Flambeau, who spoke to my youthful passion for melodrama, flamboyant gesture, special effects. Like many readers before and since, I had vainly yearned for more stories about Holmes's nemesis, the cobra-like Professor Moriarty, who really only features in "The Final Problem" and, all too tangentially, *The Valley of Fear*. Sadly, not till I was in my thirties would I discover the gentleman-thief Raffles, his French counterpart Arsène Lupin (who once opposed a certain English detective in *Arsène Lupin versus Herlock Sholmes*), and Marcel Allain and Pierre Souvestre's elusive, shape-shifting and deliciously campy Fantômas. No matter. At the age of thirteen I learned of a villain much, much worse than any of these.

One afternoon at Hills Department Store, where my mother was out trolling for bargains, I was scouring the bookshelves for "something good to read." Amid the period best sellers and self-help guides, I noticed a Pyramid paperback entitled *The Insidious Dr. Fu Manchu*. I wasn't sure what "insidious" meant, nor had I ever heard of Fu Manchu, who was resonantly described on the back cover as possessing "a brow like Shakespeare's and a face like Satan's." These days, at least, I know enough to tremble at the very sound of his name. For we are speaking here of the dreaded Yellow Peril incarnate, the greatest criminal mastermind of all time.

During the first half of the twentieth century, Sax Rohmer chronicled the Devil Doctor's repeated attempts at world domination, always through some nefarious conspiracy or diabolical stratagem. When this fiend in human form eliminated his adversaries, it was never with a mere bullet but through such sinister means as "The Call of Siva" or "The Six Gates of Joyful Wisdom." Fu's schemes, alas, were consistently thwarted by Nayland Smith, often seconded by his companion Dr. Petrie—a pair clearly modeled on Holmes and Watson. Nonetheless, the consummate Architect of Evil invariably managed to escape in each book's last chapter so that he might once again send forth his dacoits and Thuggees and Cold Men, his sheath-dressed Eurasian temptresses and all the mindless minions of the Si-Fan brotherhood.

Given their racism and xenophobia, as well as the histrionic breathlessness of Rohmer's prose and the repetitiveness of his plots, these novels are now little read except by aging nostalgicists and a few students of popular culture. I myself don't dare go back to them, lest I be seriously appalled by my youthful taste: I actually managed to ingest the complete works by the time I finished junior high, borrowing some cheap hardback editions from the mother of a school friend. Not too long ago, however, I did pick up two novels by Cay Van Ash—Rohmer's biographer and disciple—that actually pitted my hero, Sherlock Holmes, against the Chinese mastermind: *Ten Steps beyond Baker Street* and *The Fires of Fu Manchu*. Someday I'll probably give them a try.

Because the Lorain Public Library disdained to stock even Edgar Rice Burroughs's Tarzan and Mars novels, let alone Fu Manchu thrillers or obvious "pulp," I soon took to scanning the bookshelves of relatives and neighbors for possible paperback excitement, as well as regularly checking out the ever-changing book and comics racks in every drugstore in town. Like Holmes on a case, I was relentless, eventually riding my bike all over Lorain to Salvation Army and Goodwill outlets, to the St. Vincent de Paul's charity shop, to the fabulous thrift store called Clarice's Values. In one of these I discovered Howard Haycraft's *Boy's Book of Great Detective*

Stories, the precious volume in which I first read the stunning Thinking Machine classic, "The Problem of Cell 13." Who can ever forget Professor Augustus S.F.X. Van Dusen or his Houdini-like challenge to escape within seven days from a maximum security prison? " 'Suppose—just suppose—there had been no old plumbing system there?' asked the warden, curiously. 'There were two other ways out,' said The Thinking Machine, enigmatically." I can also remember enjoying, in some Literary Guild anthology or other, a story about Max Carrados—Ernest Bramah's blind detective—as well as Arthur Morrison's "The Dixon Torpedo," the best known of Martin Hewitt's cases, and at least one of the "inverse crimes" solved by the highly scientific Dr. Thorndyke of R. Austin Freeman. (The television series *Columbo* adopted this same challenging format, first showing the murder being committed, then following the detective as he gradually uncovers the truth.) Two decades later Hugh Greene, the brother of Graham, would publish four substantial collections featuring these and other late Victorian and Edwardian "rivals of Sherlock Holmes." I own mint firsts of all of them, in dust jacket.

"The Lost World"

When I reached the age of 14 or 15 someone casually mentioned that Fyodor Dostoevsky's *Crime and Punishment* was a murder mystery, so I unearthed a Bantam paperback of the Constance Garnett translation and lived in Raskolnikov's tormented soul for three glorious days. I particularly admired Dostoevsky's nightmarish intensity; every word was heavy, every action fraught. That was how I viewed my own adolescent life.

A liking for hallucinatory Russian fiction doesn't, however, preclude a lasting passion for comics, and then, as now, I particularly loved the adventures of Uncle Scrooge. More often than not, the world's richest duck, having somehow lost his immense fortune, would end up traveling to some fabled realm to retrieve it, usually with the larcenous Beagle Boys in hot pursuit. Like today's readers of Robert E. Howard and J.R.R. Tolkien, I felt strongly the allure of lost civilizations and other worlds, of faerie realms beyond the fields we know.

One evening I found myself, as so often, at Whalen's drugstore reading my way through the comics rack while trying to avoid being noticed by the gruff manager ("Hey, kid, this ain't no library!"). Suddenly, a book cover on an adjoining shelf of paperbacks caught my attention: It showed a guy on the edge of a rocky cliff, beating off a tyrannosaur with the butt end of a rifle. When I realized that the book's author was Sir Arthur Conan Doyle, I immediately plunked down my 50 cents.

Unlike the cheesy 1960 movie adaptation with the voluptuous Jill St. John (and Michael Rennie and Claude Rains), *The Lost World* (1912) doesn't feature any women on the scientific expedition up the Amazon to a plateau of Jurassic monsters and ape-men. It does open in London with the journalist-narrator Edward Malone being informed by his beloved Gladys that she will only marry a hero, but that's about it. *The Lost World* belongs squarely in that sometimes despised subgenre called "boys' adventures." Conan Doyle had thought about attempting one of these as early as 1889. That year he wrote to his mother:

> I am thinking of trying a Rider Haggardy
> kind of book called 'the Inca's Eye' dedicated
> to all the naughty boys of the Empire, by one
> who sympathizes with them. I think I could
> write a book of that sort *con amore*. . . . The

notable experiences of John H. Calder, Ivan Boscovitch, Jim Horscroft, and Major General Pengelley Jones in their search after the Inca's eye. How's that for an appetite whetter.

Conan Doyle never got any further with "The Inca's Eye," but twenty years later he renamed his quartet of heroes, retained the South American locale, and built a new plot around the latest speculations about dinosaurs and "missing links." The novel's epigraph underscores that it was still the same sort of adventure story:

I have wrought my simple plan
If I give one hour of joy
To the boy who's half a man,
Or the man who's half a boy.

To my youthful surprise, *The Lost World* wasn't just exciting, it was also funny. The squat, choleric, and heavily bristled Professor George Edward Challenger resembled "a stunted Hercules whose tremendous vitality had all run to depth, breadth, and brain." In appearance, he himself might have passed for the "missing link," a point hammered home when it turns out that Challenger could be the twin of the king of the savage ape-men. His scientific rival, the precise

Professor Summerlee, was naturally his opposite: "a tall, thin, bitter man, with the withered aspect of a theologian."

Rather than Holmes and Watson, this squabbling pair often call to mind Laurel and Hardy, or Abbott and Costello. (The vaudeville quality of their relationship is underscored in the 1925 silent film version of the novel.) Today, in fact, *The Lost World* strikes me as more comic than not, a decidedly tongue-in-cheek homage to the "boys' adventure." Little wonder that Conan Doyle actually dressed up as the heavily bearded scientist for a series of photographs, and really looks like "a primitive cave-man in a lounge suit." The writer would later choose the cantankerous Challenger as his own favorite among his characters.

Humor pervades Conan Doyle's fiction, the Baker Street saga itself being shot through with wit and gamesmanship. In one classic instance (from *The Valley of Fear*), Watson describes Moriarty as "'The famous scientific criminal, as famous among crooks as—' 'My blushes, Watson,' Holmes murmured in a deprecating voice. 'I was about to say as he is unknown to the public.'" *The Lost World*, however, approaches the distinctly slapstick. Shortly after they meet and quarrel,

Challenger locks the invasive reporter Malone in a bear hug and the two roll down the steps and out the front door and into the street. The mighty hunter Lord John Roxton speaks throughout with a silly *pukka sahib* accent and such catchphrases as "young fellah, my lad." When Malone finally returns a conquering hero, he quickly discovers that his beloved Gladys has gone and married a quite ordinary clerk named Percy Potts. No doubt the newlyweds are meant to call to mind the Pooters in George and Weedon Grossmith's contemporary satire of middle-class life, *The Diary of a Nobody*.

Far more problematic are the racial stereotypes scattered throughout *The Lost World,* a novel that already plays, uncomfortably, with the themes of evolution, atavism, and reversion to the primitive. Among the book's dramatis personae one finds easily spooked native bearers, traitorous half-breeds, and even a gigantic Negro named Zambo, ever loyal to his "Massa." Could these be intended as deliberate grotesques? Should the novel, at least in part, be reinterpreted as a satire of the boys' adventure and its colonialist conventions?

I don't propose *The Lost World* as a South American *Heart of Darkness* (published a decade earlier). Still, would the same writer who spoke so eloquently for racial tolerance in "The Yellow Face," who in his memoirs recalled with admiration his shipboard meeting with the black abolitionist Henry Highland Garnet, and who presents a harrowing account of the African American agony in his terrifying "J. Habakuk Jephson's Statement," would this same writer turn around and give us Zambo? It seems unlikely, and yet how does one then account for the surprisingly crude depiction of the Andaman Islander Tonga in *The Sign of the Four*, and the embarrassingly caricatured black boxer Steve Dixie in "The Three Gables"? There are mysteries here.

Throughout *The Lost World* the older reader, at least, will be disconcerted by the ambivalences and odd shifts in tone. Consider the virtual extermination of the ape-men. Before the novel proper begins, we learn that Lord John Roxton had once overseen a vigilante operation against the Brazilian slave trade, hunting down the slavers and coldly executing them. This aristocratic sportsman eagerly seeks opportunities to kill, judges it quite appropriate to shoot a treacherous servant, genuinely revels in the pitched battle against the ape-men, and eventually passes his bloodlust on to young Malone. Naturally, the European rifles turn the tide in the all-out war between the more "evolved" Indians and the primitive beast-men. Mass slaughter ensues. Yet look at Malone's final comment during the aftermath of this virtual genocide:

> At the end of the victorious campaign the surviving ape-folk were driven across the plateau (their wailings were horrible) and established in the neighborhood of the Indian caves, where they would, from now onwards, be a servile race under the eyes of their masters. It was a rude, raw, primeval version of the Jews in Babylon or the Israelites in Egypt. At night we could hear from amid the trees the long-drawn cry, as some primitive Ezekiel mourned for fallen greatness and recalled the departed glories of Ape Town. Hewers of wood and drawers of water, such were they from now onwards.

What are we to make of this elevated biblical language? One might argue that the passage uncomfortably likens the Jews to a lower form of humanity. Yet its obvious poetry transmutes the ape-men into tragic victims of history. Throughout this novel Conan Doyle consistently overturns expectations, repeatedly mingling humor and horror, satire and pathos.

At the end of *The Lost World*, Conan Doyle strongly suggests the likelihood of a sequel. On the last page, after all, Malone and Roxton are already planning a new expedition to Maple White Land, the name they had given the plateau. As a boy, I imagined titles like "Return to the Lost World," while picturing further adventures among the pterodactyls and tyrannosaurs. But there were no further Challenger adventures listed in the public library's card catalog. All I could do was wait and hope that one day. . . .

Thus it was that several years went by before I happened upon a copy of *The Poison Belt* (1913) in a Mexico City bazaar, during a post–high-school graduation road trip. It was a relatively chintzy paperback and also included the two late Challenger short stories, "When the World Screamed" (1928) and "The Disintegration Machine" (1929). I opened the book with considerable anticipation.

Certainly, *The Poison Belt* begins well, neatly blending the familiar bluster, slapstick, and suspense. Professor Challenger has sent the *Daily Gazette* a letter alerting the public to a vague cosmic danger approaching the earth. Malone, Summerlee, and Roxton are then all invited to the Challenger country home and ordered, without explanation, to bring along oxygen canisters. En route, Conan Doyle quietly suggests that all is not quite right with the world—automobile drivers behave with strange carelessness, people on the street start fistfights over nothing, and even the stern Professor Summerlee seems out of character, suddenly announcing that he possesses rare skills as a mimic of barnyard animals:

"You know me as the austere man of science. Can you believe that I once had a well-deserved reputation in several nurseries as a farmyard imitator? Perhaps I can help you to pass the time in a pleasant way. Would it amuse you to hear me crow like a cock?"

"No, sir," said Lord John, who was still greatly offended; "it would *not* amuse me."

"My imitation of the clucking hen who had just laid an egg was also considered rather above the average. Might I venture?"

"No, sir, no—certainly not."

But, in spite of this earnest prohibition, Professor Summerlee laid down his pipe and for the rest of our journey he entertained—or failed to entertain—us by a succession of bird and animal cries. . . .

What is happening to everyone? All grows clear when Challenger announces that the earth has just entered an interstellar "poison belt" and that all animal life is doomed. Perhaps the most dryly witty exchange in all of Conan Doyle occurs next. Challenger thanks his butler for his long and faithful service, then explains:

> "I'm expecting the end of the world today, Austin."
> "Yes, sir. What time, sir?"
> "I can't say, Austin. Before evening."
> "Very good, sir."
> The taciturn Austin saluted and withdrew.

Here, surely, is one inspiration behind the imperturbable Jeeves of Conan Doyle's best student, P. G. Wodehouse.

Only the four friends, and Mrs. Challenger, possess sufficient oxygen to live on for a day or so, coolly observing the gradual devastation of our planet. As predicted, the unprepared world quickly succumbs to the deadly "daturon" gas, with "the less developed races" being "the first to respond to its influence." Trains crash when the drivers lose consciousness, fires break out everywhere (New York is destroyed), children are found dead outside their schools, and birds clutter the ground. Uncanny silence blankets the earth.

Alas, in the manner of those Gothic novels that eventually present rational explanations for seemingly spectral happenings or suddenly reveal that the clanking horror was only a trick, Conan Doyle can't quite follow through with his stark vision of the apocalypse: Instead, it turns out that the cosmic poison hasn't inflicted death but merely catalepsy, and, after a day of unconsciousness, everyone wakes up, resuming their tasks without any memory of the lost hours.

The Poison Belt is less a "boys' adventure" or even an early example of British science-fictional disaster fiction (like H. G. Wells' similar *In the Days of the Comet*) than a moralist's parable, at times a quite moving philosophical dialogue. During their supposed last hours, the argumentative friends debate the meaning of life and whether the spirit might survive the body. Here Conan Doyle's life-long fascination with spiritual—or Spiritualist—matters starts to develop a shrill stridency. As Challenger contends:

> "Nature may build a beautiful door and hang it with many a gauzy and shimmering curtain to make an entrance to the new life for our

wondering souls. . . . No, Summerlee, I will have none of your materialism, for I, at least, am too great a thing to end in mere physical constituents, a packet of salts and three bucketfuls of water. Here—here"—and he beat his great head with his huge, hairy fist—"there is something which uses matter, but is not of it— something which might destroy death, which Death can never destroy."

Later on, Challenger further sermonizes:

"As to the body . . . we do not mourn over the parings of our nails nor the cut locks of our hair, though they were once part of ourselves. Neither does a one-legged man yearn sentimentally over his missing member. The physical body has rather been a source of pain and fatigue to us. It is the constant index of our limitations. Why then should we worry about the detachment from our psychical selves?"

But, as Summerlee points out, can our psychical selves actually be "detached" from our bodies?

"The Great Awakening"—as the novel's theologically suggestive final chapter is called—refers not only to the revival of the earth's inhabitants, but also to a spiritual-social revolution. Because of a universal near-death experience, "what will not be forgotten, and what will and should continue to obsess our imaginations, is this revelation of the possibilities of the universe, this destruction of our ignorant self-complacency, and this demonstration of how narrow is the path of our material existence, and what abysses may lie upon either side of it." Here, surely, Conan Doyle is suggesting that there's more to life than meets the eye and that we should pay attention to our oft-maligned seers and psychic explorers of the unknown.

At seventeen I simply found all these metaphysical passages boring and the novel rather a sad letdown. There was, for one thing, altogether too much conversation, and my overall disappointment—the first awakening of the critical faculty—was capped by the didactic ending. Now, however, *The Poison Belt* seems far more attractive, the silliness even funnier than I remember it, the philosophical speculations surprisingly touching and human. What's more, the novel concludes with a Utopian vision of a new heaven and a new earth, albeit one paid for by increased taxes. As Malone writes:

Surely we are agreed that the more sober and restrained pleasures of the present are deeper as well as wiser than the noisy, foolish hustle which passed so often for enjoyment in the days of old—days so recent and yet already so inconceivable. Those empty lives which were wasted in aimless visiting and being visited, in the worry of great and unnecessary households, in the arranging and eating of elaborate and tedious meals, have now found rest and health in the reading, the music, the gentle family communion which comes from a simpler and saner division of their time. With greater health and greater pleasure they are richer than before, even after they have paid those increased contributions to the common fund which have so raised the standard of life in these islands.

"When the World Screamed"—the first of two short Challenger adventures—displays its own talkiness and didacticism. Conan Doyle was apparently convinced that an almost Zolaesque description of the digging of a tunnel deep into the earth would prove utterly enthralling to the ordinary reader. Yet the central idea behind the story strikingly recalls the Gaia thesis: Challenger maintains that "the world upon which we live is itself a living organism, endowed, as I believe, with a circulation, a respiration, and a nervous system of its own." If we prick such an animate earth, will it not bleed, will it not howl in pain?

The other Challenger short story, "The Disintegration Machine," starts well, then quickly becomes a science fictional jape, a sour *jeu d'esprit*. Still, it opens with a priceless demonstration of the burly professor's majestic egotism: By now, Conan Doyle's readers can relish the irascible Challenger's vanity as much as they do Sherlock Holmes's penchant for wowing Watson with his seemingly uncanny deductions. Challenger is commenting on one of Malone's articles:

> "You began a paragraph with the words: 'Professor G.E. Challenger, who is among our greatest living scientists—'"
>
> "Well, sir?" I asked.
>
> "Why these invidious qualifications and limitations? Perhaps you can mention who these other predominant scientific men may be to whom you impute equality, or possibly superiority to myself?"
>
> "It was badly worded . . . ."

"My dear young friend, do not imagine that I am exacting, but surrounded as I am by pugnacious and unreasonable colleagues, one is forced to take one's own part. Self-assertion is foreign to my nature, but I have to hold my ground against opposition."

In the story proper a scientist has invented a ray that can dissolve a body into its component atoms—and, if so desired, then reassemble them. Challenger and Malone learn that the machine has been sold to a dangerous foreign power. In the end, the patriotic professor turns the ray on its inventor to prevent such a terrible weapon from being loosed upon the world. Challenger dismisses his cold-blooded murder by resorting to the jejune morality of the "first strike": He has simply done away with a man who would have vaporized thousands or millions of people. One can almost hear the sanctimonious whisper, "The end justifies the means."

Of course, being by this time a convinced Spiritualist, Conan Doyle no longer viewed death as entirely horrible or, indeed, even as death. Life continued on the Other Side. The writer could actually accept with relative equanimity the death of his oldest son at the very end of World War I—indeed, he was able to give a Spiritualist speech shortly after he heard the news because of his confidence that we survive our physical bodies. Thus in *The Land of Mist* (1926)—the last and least read of the five Challenger stories—Malone, Challenger's daughter Enid, and the hardheaded professor himself are all converted to Spiritualism.

The novel opens by underscoring Challenger's sorrow over the deaths of his wife and Professor Summerlee. He is now, however, resolutely anti-Spiritualist, asserting that he really is just "four buckets of water and a bagful of salts." Recall that Challenger had employed much the same colorful phrase in *The Poison Belt*, at that time insisting that he was much *more* than his physical body; here he reverses the meaning and reverts to strict materialism. (One might also note that the good professor seems to have put on some weight, being now four, rather than three, bucketsful of water.)

While episodic and tendentious, *The Land of Mist* does offer some excellent glimpses of lower-middle-class London life, somewhat in the vein of the social novels of George Gissing and H. G. Wells. It is also, like several earlier books, in particular *The Stark Munro Letters*, strongly autobiographical and openly concerned with religious doubt and the search for belief. Yet failing a strong plot or the concision required by the short story, Conan Doyle's fiction always runs the risk of becoming talky, of transforming what should be a romance into "a course of lectures."

Looking over the whole Challenger saga, it's clear that all the adventures turn, more or less, on the divide between higher and lower, between the spiritual and the material. As early as *The Lost World,* Conan Doyle had broached this theme when discussing Malone's psychic sensitivity—due to his Celtic heritage—and the possible existence of "telepathy." *The Poison Belt* is essentially a modern symposium about life after death. "When the World Screamed" reveals that even the inorganic world is more alive than it seems, and "The Disintegration Machine" demonstrates that people can be disembodied and yet continue to live. *The Land of Mist* is, finally, a full-scale exploration of the relationship between the palpable and the immaterial. It was, Conan Doyle said, the "big psychic novel" he had longed to write and "was to me so important that I feared I might pass away before it was finished." Like the elderly Tolstoy, who preferred his late religious writings to *Anna Karenina*, Conan Doyle ultimately judged the message of Spiritualism as far more important than merely telling a good story. We all make mistakes.

"Twilight Tales"

In *The Lost World*, Malone's editor McArdle tells him, "The big blank spaces in the map are all being filled in, and there's no room for romance anywhere." But what boy, or girl, reads for anything but mystery, excitement, and romance? Hence my own youthful passion for Alexandre Dumas's *The Count of Monte Cristo* and Rider Haggard's *King Solomon's Mines*, not to mention my perfect willingness to forgo all homework to finish Jules Verne's *Journey to the Center of the Earth, Twenty Thousand Leagues under the Sea*, or *The Mysterious Island*. From such undisputed classics of adventure I naturally advanced to the high spots of golden-age science fiction, fantasy, and horror. By the time I graduated from high school I was regularly seeking out collections of eerie tales—and in many of them I discovered stories by A. Conan Doyle.

All too often posterity remembers some authors, no matter how multifaceted their genius, for only one or two books. Who, aside from scholars of Victorian fiction, now reads anything by Thackeray other than *Vanity Fair*? *Jane Eyre* has largely driven out Charlotte Bronte's great depiction of loneliness, *Villette*. From early on the worldwide popularity of Sherlock Holmes annoyed his creator, and with some cause: The detective's adventures, wonderful as they are, tended to overshadow everything else Conan Doyle ever wrote, with the partial exception of *The Lost World*. Yet the gothic elements that recur throughout the Holmes canon—in "The Speckled Band," *The Hound of the Baskervilles*, "The Creeping Man," and elsewhere—at least remind us that Arthur Conan Doyle is also a major figure in the history of the weird tale.

Today much of Conan Doyle's substantial oeuvre—his bibliography runs to over 700 pages—suffers readerly neglect because of the widespread misconception that he only rose above the conventions of his time when he wrote about the dynamic duo of Baker Street. His other works are consequently dismissed as period pieces, of interest mainly to professional Doyleans. For instance, it's commonly assumed that historical novels like *Micah Clarke* or *Sir Nigel* must be, at best, fustian, pseudo-antiquarian homages to Walter Scott—and nobody bothers with Scott any more, let alone his imitators. Tales of prizefighting like "The

Croxley Master" or stories of late Victorian medical life such as those gathered in *Round the Red Lamp* merely sound dated or unappealing. Wrong on both counts.

Besides, even when a work *is* dated, that's not necessarily a bad thing, as Baker Street's gaslight and hansom cab atmosphere reminds us again and again. Some of Conan Doyle's "twilight tales," as he once planned to title an early collection of eerie stories, can stand up to the best work of such masters of the uncanny as Sheridan Le Fanu and M. R. James. To my taste, "The Captain of the *Pole-Star*" (1883) ranks second only to Vernon Lee's seductive and unsettling "*Amour Dure*" as the most poetic of Victorian ghost stories. In this, Conan Doyle's very first masterpiece, a ship sailing into the ice floes of the north is haunted by something elusive that roams the deck at night, softly moaning, but never quite glimpsed by anyone except the ship's commander. As the Sherlockian and ghost-story scholar Barbara Roden points out, there are echoes throughout this poignant tale—a ghost story that is also a love story—of *Wuthering Heights* as well as of *Frankenstein*. Rather than reveal any more of the plot, let me just recommend that you read it or even, to paraphrase the lingo of the poker player, "Read it and weep."

Like "The Captain of the *Pole-Star*," many of Conan Doyle's weird tales espouse an almost documentary *verismo*, often through the use of diaries and letters. Alternately, they adopt the style of the after-dinner reminiscence, like those so-called "club tales" in which some elderly duffer takes a sip at his whiskey and murmurs, "Did you say ancient idols? That reminds me of rather a rum thing that happened when I was young. Out East, don't you know. . . ."

Today an attentive Conan Doyle reader might occasionally guess a story's plot twist, usually because its narrative tricks and switchbacks have been adopted by others. In "The Great Keinplatz Experiment," for instance, one recognizes what is now a commonplace of science-fictional farce: the exchange of souls (compare, for instance, F. Anstey's *Vice-Versa*, P. G. Wodehouse's *Laughing Gas*, and movies like *Freaky Friday*). But even here we happily read on, eager to see how Conan Doyle works out a screwball comedy that flirts with possible incest while also suggesting what would be—as H. G. Wells recognized in "The Story of the Late Mr. Elvesham"—a surefire, if immensely cruel, system for attaining immortality.

Like Guy de Maupassant, whom he greatly admired (and learned from), Conan Doyle almost always moves his stories right along, and seldom repeats himself in his choice of subject. He typically captures the reader's attention with a premonitory opening sentence: "Of the dealings of Edward Bellingham with William Monkhouse Lee, and of the cause of the great terror of Abercrombie Smith, it may be that no absolute and final judgment will ever be delivered." So begins "Lot No. 249," perhaps his most anthologized tale of the uncanny. Together with "The Ring of Thoth" (which mixes elements of Rider Haggard's immortal *She* with eschatological reflections about life without death), "Lot No. 249" almost certainly inspired the 1930s Boris Karloff film *The Mummy* and thus an entire subgenre of film horror. I envy anyone who has yet to read it.

While virtually anything Conan Doyle produced is likely to be absorbing, four or five of his works of the grotesque and supernatural are astonishingly original, providing far more than just careful plotting, a mesmerizing narrator, or a shocker ending. Is there a more physical ghost in the literature than the antagonist in "The Bully of Brocas Court" (1921) or a more stomach-churning "psychic" chiller than "The Leather Funnel" (1903)? Certainly no one ever forgets the gruesome climax of "The Case of Lady Sannox"

(1893) in which a doctor reluctantly performs a disfiguring operation on a veiled Muslim woman. The innocuous-sounding "J. Habakuk Jephson's Statement" (1884)—Conan Doyle's second short masterpiece—is as troubling as Melville's "Benito Cereno," and arguably even more shocking.

Two superb later "creepers," as their author sometimes dubbed such work, "The Terror of Blue John Gap" (1910) and "The Horror of the Heights" (1913), deal, in their turn, with what one might call "monsters of the id." The first of these focuses on a primordial (and ultimately pitiable) Thing that emerges from deep within the earth. Yet is this shadowy cave creature truly a survival from eons past? Or does it actually emerge from deep within the narrator's sick and troubled mind? As with so many tales of the uncanny, there is room for either explanation.

"The Horror of the Heights" I first read as a boy, and I remember being long troubled by the fear that the life-giving air around me might actually be inhabited by bloodthirsty creatures. The story itself takes the form of a logbook kept by a noted "aeronaut" named Joyce-Armstrong who has become obsessed with flying into the upper reaches of the atmosphere. From the start Conan Doyle works hard to establish the bona fides of his tale: In his first two paragraphs he mentions six proper names, several geographical sites—such as Lower Haycock, Chauntry Farm, and the Flying School on Salisbury Plain—as well as the past history and present London location of a bloodstained notebook, an artifact that the curious might presumably examine were they to visit the Aero Club. Only when the tale has been sufficiently "framed," so that the reader has been given every reason to believe what follows to be verifiable fact, only then does Conan Doyle transcribe Joyce-Armstrong's narrative.

But just beforehand, he builds some additional suspense by mentioning a few striking personal details about his subject. Joyce-Armstrong, we are told, usually carried a shotgun in his cockpit, and regularly hinted that he knew something unsettling about certain mysterious plane crashes. We learn that this fearless pilot was "a poet and a dreamer, as well as a mechanic and an inventor." In part, "The Horror of the Heights" exploits this tension between the clear-sighted and the starry-eyed.

Jules Verne—whose work, in French, the young Conan Doyle devoured—made sure that his *voyages extraordinaires* were always grounded in a comparable abundance of factual detail, not only to add credibility to a strange tale but also to instruct his readers in the latest developments in contemporary technology or science. Similarly, when Joyce-Armstrong begins his exploration of the higher reaches of the atmosphere, he first expounds the virtues of the monoplane over the biplane, mentions the quietness of his new improved motor, and listens attentively to the hum of its ten spark plugs. His is very much the voice of the practical, down-to-earth engineer.

Yet as Joyce-Armstrong ascends into the outer limits, he grows ever more lyrical in his descriptions of clouds, hail showers, and windstorms, despite the intense cold and an increased sense of deadly solitude. His exhilaration might be aptly called rapture of the heights. As a result, when the aeronaut first glimpses the giant floating jellyfish, he reacts to them as would a Wordsworth or Shelley of the stratosphere: They strike him as sublime, awe-inspiring creatures of visionary grandeur, "bell-shaped and of enormous size—far larger, I should judge, than the dome of St. Paul's." Yet "there was in them a delicacy of texture and colouring which reminded me of the finest Venetian glass. Pale shades of pink and green were the prevailing tints, but all had a lovely iridescence where the sun shimmered through their dainty forms."

Vision is, in fact, central to "The Horror of the Heights." Joyce-Armstrong precisely chronicles what he observes on his ascent—the appearance of the English landscape, birds, other planes, meteorites. He describes the fogging of his goggles by the rain, as well as his great desire simply to catch sight of one of his suspected monsters of the air. First our hero detects "a fine diaphanous vapour drifting" around him, then the air loses its "crystal clearness. It was full of long, ragged wisps of something which I can only compare to very fine cigarette-smoke. It hung in wreaths and coils, turning and twisting slowly in the sunlight." The dirigible-sized jellyfish are likened to floating soap bubbles, then are succeeded by the vapor-like "air-snakes," which dart so quickly "that the eyes could hardly follow them." Their outline is "hazy" but they are "very light grey or smoke colour, with some darker lines within." Even the huge, malevolent "purple horrors" that later threaten Joyce-Armstrong are fundamentally diaphanous.

To me, Joyce-Armstrong's aerial visions are hardly all that unusual: I began to see them about the time I first read the story, and I've now grown used to them. Middle-aged sight is flecked with what are commonly called "floaters," translucent wisps and small discolorations that zigzag across the field of vision. Ophthalmologists are always asked about them, and without reassurance the first appearance of floaters can inspire real fear of incipient blindness. That young eye doctor, Arthur Conan Doyle—for ophthalmology was his eventual specialty—must have heard many descriptions of these gelatinous, curlicue invaders hovering in the air before his worried patients' eyes. The horrors of the heights resemble such creatures writ large, very large. Indeed, to be only slightly fanciful, if one regards the earth as a gigantic pupil, then the air-monsters of the upper cloudland are floaters in the surrounding white of the eye.

Joyce-Armstrong's sight may be responsible for these glaucous creatures in yet an even more common manner: The narrative leaves open the possibility that the pilot may actually be hallucinating, creating nightmares out of puffs of floating water vapor. The empty desert generates mirages—why not the empty atmosphere? We all tend to see what we look for. Besides, who has not noticed, after some quick turning of the head, an occasional flash of something light or dark, just on the edge of the field of vision?

The particular structure of "The Horror of the Heights" precludes much real suspense about its outcome—to slightly modify the title of a Yeats poem, "An English Airman Foresees His Death." But as a text it is surprisingly rich in archetypal associations, suggesting the twinship of the atmosphere with the ocean, implicitly likening the gigantic "purple horror" that seeks to engulf Joyce-Armstrong to a supersized *vagina dentata*, and even calling to mind the ectoplasmic discharges so common at the séances that would soon obsess their author.

While Conan Doyle's eerie tales are at their very least accomplished period pieces, several stand out for their disturbingly modern suggestiveness. I'm thinking, in particular, of "John Barrington Cowles" and "The Parasite," two tales of sexual perversity and obsession. The first depicts a "Belle Dame Sans Merci" who fascinates, then destroys the three men she enthralls. In each case, shortly before a much-anticipated wedding, Miss Northcott discloses something about herself and makes a request of her fiancé. Conan Doyle leaves unsaid what she reveals or asks. Could she be some sort of lamia, not wholly human? A vampire? An agent of the devil? In every case, the men ultimately prefer death to her company—and yet all announce that no matter what they do, they can neither stop loving her nor escape her.

The novella-length "The Parasite" explores some of the same themes as "John Barrington Cowles." A young scientist falls under the psychological control of a crippled, unattractive woman possessed of extraordinary mesmeric influence. Miss Penclosa soon compels young Professor Gilroy to profess love for her, even though her physical person thoroughly repels him. Yet he is slavishly drawn back to kneel at her feet again and again. At one point, Gilroy, manipulated by the jealous medium, actually prepares to throw acid into the face of his beautiful fiancée Agatha. Beneath the overt metaphor of hypnotic power, Conan Doyle hints at our inner darkness and the addictive thrills of sexual transgression.

Like several other early works, "The Parasite" also proffers echoes or prefigurations of Baker Street. For instance, revenge through acid disfigurement dramatically reappears in "The Illustrious Client." Even more strikingly, Professor Gilroy often sounds very much like the great detective. "Surmise and fancy," proudly records the scientist in his journal, "have no place in my scheme of thought. Show me what I can see with my microscope, cut with my scalpel, weigh in my balance, and I will devote a lifetime to its investigation. But when you ask me to study feelings, impressions, suggestions, you ask me to do what is distasteful and even demoralizing. A departure from pure reason affects me like an evil smell or a musical discord." As it happens, Professor Gilroy will soon be doing a great deal that his conscious mind finds "distasteful and even demoralizing."

Despite its bland title, "Uncle Jeremy's Household" is a highly atmospheric mystery-thriller that also strikes several Holmesian, and sometimes Hitchcockian, notes. Reminiscent of *The Sign of the Four*, but far more shocking, its plot embraces a lonely household, an Anglo-Indian governess, several deaths, and apparent blackmail, the whole story being marked by an intense eroticism and hints of atavistic savagery. The narrator, who resides in Baker Street, is the scientific Hugh Lawrence; he has a John H. Watson–like friend named . . . John H. Thurston.

Puzzled by the mysterious governess, Lawrence decides "to study her as an entomologist might study a specimen, critically, but without bias." He insists that he himself feels no attraction for Miss Warrender: "I look on her as an interesting psychological problem, nothing more." She turns out to be far more than just an interesting psychological problem. "Uncle Jeremy's

Household" is just one of the many first-rate early tales—another is "The Recollections of Captain Willkie," about a raffish con artist—unearthed and reprinted by John Michael Gibson and Richard Lancelyn Green in *The Unknown Conan Doyle: Uncollected Stories by Arthur Conan Doyle*. Nearly all are immensely readable and very few dismissable as mere juvenilia.

Of even greater interest to Sherlockians are two of Conan Doyle's "round the fire stories" (the title of the 1908 collection in which they were later included). Both, first published when Holmes was supposedly dead, poke gentle fun at the master detective. In "The Man with the Watches," a corpse is found on a train in what is essentially a locked room murder; in "The Lost Special," an entire train and its five passengers disappear. The crimes seem impossible, even supernatural. Yet "an amateur reasoner of some celebrity" writes to *The Times* with proposed solutions to each. The voice of the correspondent is unmistakable:

> It is one of the elementary principles of practical reasoning that when the impossible has been eliminated the residuum, *however improbable*, must contain the truth. . . .

As it happens, this solemn-sounding and well-known "criminal investigator" is wildly wrong in both cases. We learn what really happened through letters received, many years later, from the people involved. Despite adopting this feeble and lackluster way of ultimately explaining the puzzles, "The Man with the Watches" and "The Lost Special" are excellent howdunits, especially enjoyable in their opening pages when everything seems inexplicable. That hint of the supernatural adds just the right flavor.

Much as I loved Conan Doyle's tales of the fantastic and uncanny, they were hard to find. I would always look for A. Conan Doyle in genre anthologies—especially those innumerable "Alfred Hitchcock" collections, all bearing titles like *Stories That Scared Even Me*—but would generally settle for anything by a small handful of writers who fed my hunger for the sardonic, witty, and unsettling: John Collier, Jack Finney, Fredric Brown, Roald Dahl, C. L. Moore, Gerald Kersh, Avram Davidson, and—still with us as I write in 2011—Ray Bradbury. But above them all stood Edward John Moreton Drax Plunkett, 18th Baron of Dunsany (1878–1957). What Conan Doyle is to the detective story, Lord Dunsany is to the modern fantasy: the Master.

One study hall period at Admiral King High School I was poking around the small travel section of the school library when I noticed a book entitled *Jorkens Remembers Africa*. Suspecting it to be some Great White Hunter's gung-ho memoir about the fierce man-eaters he had killed, I half-heartedly plucked the book from the shelf. On the title page was a small illustration, revealing a hunter in deadly combat with . . . a unicorn. Recognizing that here was a book that had been seriously misshelved, I immediately signed it out.

Lord Dunsany, like Sir Arthur, wrote easily and he wrote a lot. Some people find his early prose over rich, far too ornate and redolent of the *fin de siècle*. But Dunsany soon tamped down his youthful excesses. What could be simpler or more striking than the opening to "The Hoard of the Gibbelins"? "The Gibbelins eat, as is well known, nothing less good than man." While I revere all of Dunsany, his many Jorkens stories—there are six volumes—possess something of the same compulsive readability as the Sherlock Holmes adventures.

Related as he sits by the fire in the Billiards Club, Jorkens's anecdotes are tall tales about mermaids and ancient curses and trees that walk, about a diamond bigger than the Ritz and an unexpected trip to Mars. All these improbable stories are related in a perfectly serious tone, usually with an air of distinct wistfulness. There's certainly no way to prove or disprove them:

> The talk had veered round to runes and curses and witches, one bleak December evening, where a few of us sat warm in easy chairs round the cheery fire of the Billiards Club. "Do you believe in witches?" one of us said to Jorkens. "It isn't what I believe in that matters so much," said Jorkens, "Only what I have seen."

Now old, fat, and always in need of a fresh drink, Jorkens looks back with nostalgia on his youth when the world was full of those "big blank spaces" McArdle had spoken of in *The Lost World*. In the past, or at least in Jorkens's past, you could travel to Africa, or Russia, or any of the distant parts of the British Empire, and just naturally fall into something a bit out of the way. The world was a realm of marvels. Once, for instance, Jorkens found himself surrounded by African warriors who dressed—well, let him tell it:

> "Eighty-five men with spears, of a tribe that I did not know, and every one of them in evening dress. . . . White ties, white waistcoats,"

said Jorkens quietly. "In fact just what you are wearing now, except that they had rather heavier watch-chains, and they all wore diamond solitaires."

After allowing this image to take hold for a moment, the storyteller quickly adds:

"And the first thing I thought was that I need hardly expect the worst, because however nasty the spears looked, anything like cannibalism was impossible in decent evening dress, such as they were all wearing. I was wrong there."

Jorkens's very best reminiscences blend that touch of humor with something more: horror in "The Walk to Lingham," mystery in "Ozymandias," science fiction in "Our Distant Cousins," and, most often of all, vanished romance, especially in "A Mystery of the East" and the bittersweet mermaid tale, "Mrs. Jorkens." In reading such stories, anyone of a certain age will experience the distinctive heartache that accompanies the remembrance of things past:

Then all the loneliness came back to me, all the bleak emptiness there in the world when mystery has left it, and all the aching of my heart for magic, or whatever it is that puts a wonder upon whatever it touches, and cannot itself be described.

I mention my discovery of, and pleasure in, Dunsany for a couple of reasons. Gradually, I was becoming aware that in one generation—in effect, during the lifetime of Arthur Conan Doyle—there appeared most of our pattern-establishing masterpieces of science fiction, horror, fantasy, and adventure. Recall just some of the English-language books published in the forty years between 1885 and 1925: *King Solomon's Mines, Kidnapped, The Prisoner of Zenda, The Time Machine, Dracula, Kim, The Scarlet Pimpernel, Five Children and It, Peter Pan, The Picture of Dorian Gray, The Man Who Was Thursday, Tarzan of the Apes, Flatland, The Thirty-Nine Steps, Ghost Stories of an Antiquary, The War of the Worlds, Trent's Last Case, Riders of the Purple Sage, The Wind in the Willows, Captain Blood,* and dozens of others.

But I also bring up Dunsany's Jorkens stories because Conan Doyle himself produced his own series of improbable "club tales," though his emphasize history and narrow escapes rather than mystery and magic. In fact some readers believe that the writer's finest set of short stories are, *pace* Holmes, the two volumes devoted to the recollections of an old Napoleonic soldier: *The Exploits of Brigadier Gerard* (1896) and *The Adventures of Gerard* (1903). They are, in novelist George Mac-Donald Fraser's summary, "a splendid catalog of secret missions, escapes, love affairs, duels, disguises, pursuits, triumphs, and occasional disasters," all of them related in an "inimitable mock French style." Their rumbustious gusto clearly helped inspire Fraser's own brilliant historical novels about Harry Flashman, but unlike that irrepressible Victorian cad and coward, Etienne Gerard is one of the most endearing and honorable figures in all of literature.

The Brigadier is also comically naïve, charmingly vain, and absolutely convinced that every woman finds him irresistible. After all, is he not the finest horseman and greatest swordsman in all of France? "Everybody," he reminds us, "had heard of me since my duel with the six fencing-masters." Now an old man, he sits in a café, "between his dinner and his dominoes," sipping his glass of Burgundy or Bordeaux, recalling—sometimes with a heavy heart—the glorious days of his youth.

Gerard, it would appear, seems to have been regularly summoned by Napoleon whenever desperate times called for the most desperate measures. Threats to the Emperor's life? Imperial orders that must be carried through enemy lines? State documents to be safeguarded from traitors? An arsenal inside a besieged city that needs to be blown up? Etienne Gerard is obviously the only man for the job.

Sometimes the Brigadier's reminiscences do read almost too much like tall tales, and events invariably grow madcap whenever our hero encounters the English. This blithely unaware French soldier never quite understands these foreigners and their strange sports and games, but is nonetheless unshakably certain that he possesses a natural talent, indeed an inherent superiority, at cricket and fox hunting. "How the Brigadier Slew the Fox" is a long-established classic of humorous misunderstanding. Yet other reminiscences, such as "How the Brigadier Rode to Minsk" and "How the Brigadier Captured Saragossa," are thrilling, frenzied with action, and occasionally even horrifying, as when Gerard discovers that the Spanish have nailed a French spy, alive, to a convent wall. (Mickey Spillane would later adopt this same method of restraint in one of his Mike

Hammer mysteries.) Moreover, Gerard assures us that we, to our good fortune, are the first, the very first, "save for two or three men and a score or two of women," to hear these unrivaled tales of derring-do.

A score or two of women? Like any Gascon worth his salt, Gerard is not only fierce and handsome, he loves the ladies—and is soft putty in their hands, though he seldom realizes it. He and his brigade of hussars, he proudly maintains, "could set a whole population running, the women towards us, and the men away." Once disguised as a Cossack and threatened with capture by Prussian troops, he shouts out the only Russian words he knows. "I learned them from little Sophie, at Wilna, and they meant: 'If the night is fine we shall meet under the oak tree, and if it rains we shall meet in the byre.'" Still, Gerard is more Cyrano than Don Juan, and he looks back at his youthful romantic adventures with gratitude:

> And even as they spoke I saw her in front of us, her sweet face framed in the darkness. I had cause to hate her, for she had cheated and befooled me, and yet it thrilled me then and thrills me now to think that my arms have em-

braced her, and that I have felt the scent of her hair in my nostrils. I know not whether she lies under her German earth, or whether she still lingers, a grey-haired woman in her Castle of Hof, but she lives ever, young and lovely, in the heart and the memory of Etienne Gerard.

Over the course of these stories, Conan Doyle gradually presents a warts-and-all portrait of Napoleon, at the same time making clear the Emperor's charisma and the almost rapt devotion of his soldiers. However, the villains are my favorite characters in the *Exploits* and *Adventures*; they are never quite what you expect. When the captured Brigadier is led into the cave headquarters of one Spanish guerrilla leader, the bloodthirsty monster turns out to resemble a benign *père de famille*, seated among his papers, pen in hand. He hardly notices Gerard at first, so intent is his concentration. "'I suppose,' said he, at last, speaking very excellent French, 'that you are not able to suggest a rhyme for the word Covillha.'" When Gerard finally hunts down another freebooter known as the Marechal de Millefleurs, the scoundrel turns out to be a model of gentlemanly courtesy and nonchalance, even in the face of imminent death: "The Marshal, still pinioned, and with the rope round his neck, sat his horse with a half smile, as one who is slightly bored and yet strives out of courtesy not to show it." It might be the actor Jeremy Irons at his most disdainful and world-weary.

Gerard's heroic deeds embrace the entire history and geography of the Napoleonic Wars, taking place in France, Italy, Spain, Portugal, Germany, Russia, England, and, finally, on St. Helena. No matter where he finds himself, however, the Brigadier always thinks like a hussar: "Of all the cities which we visited Venice is the most ill-built and ridiculous. I cannot imagine how the people who laid it out thought that the cavalry could maneuver." As for Waterloo, that plain of sorrows, he writes: "On the one side, poetry, gallantry, self-sacrifice—all that is beautiful and heroic. On the other side, beef. Our hopes, our ideals, our dreams—all were shattered on that terrible beef of Old England."

While Brigadier Gerard will never become a living myth like Holmes, his *Exploits* and *Adventures* really shouldn't be missed. They are, in the view of historian Owen Dudley Edwards, "the greatest historical short story series" of all time, as well as a brilliant evocation of the Napoleonic ethos. "You have seen through my dim eyes," the old soldier reminds us, "something of the sparkle and splendour of those great days, and I have brought back to you some shadow of those men whose tread shook the earth. Treasure it in your minds and pass it on to your children, for the memory of a great age is the most precious treasure that a nation can possess." *Vive l'Empereur!*

"Steel True, Blade Straight"

From his earliest schooldays Arthur Conan Doyle possessed an almost preternatural gift for storytelling. He once recalled his talent as a youthful talespinner in his essay, "Juvenilia." On a "wet half-holiday," he would stand on a desk, with classmates squatting on the floor all around him, and talk himself "husky over the misfortunes of my heroes," sometimes pausing at the very height of the action until he was bribed to continue with pastries or apples:

> When I had got as far as "With his left hand in her glossy locks, he was waving the blood-stained knife above her head, when—" or "Slowly, slowly, the door turned upon its hinges, and with eyes which were dilated with

horror, the wicked Marquis saw—" I knew that I had my audience in my power.

Perhaps because thrilling narrative came easily to him, Conan Doyle never quite valued the Sherlock Holmes and Gerard stories, let alone his ghostly tales, as they deserve. Instead he himself was convinced that his best books were (1) his medieval historical novel *The White Company* and its prequel *Sir Nigel*; (2) his multivolume history of World War I; and (3) his writings about Spiritualism.

What do these disparate works have in common, other than being generally ignored by most modern readers? All of them are, more or less, tendentious; in other words, they were written with an instructive purpose. When speaking of the merits of *The White Company*, Conan Doyle didn't point to its humor, battles, and word-painting, but instead stressed that it would "illuminate our national traditions."

To this child of the Victorian era and product of a stern Jesuit education, the supreme function of literature was to inspire men—he was less concerned about women—and to inspire them to become paragons of chivalric virtue: brave, courteous, heroic, trustworthy, stoic, self-controlled, sportsmanlike. Given the run of a large library, Conan Doyle confesses (in *Through the Magic Door)*, he almost always picks out "a book of soldier memoirs. Man is never so interesting as when he is thoroughly in earnest, and no one is so earnest as he whose life is at stake upon the event."

Throughout his own packed life the most popular writer since Dickens repeatedly sought out occasions to test his mettle, often while decked out in some kind of homemade uniform. He once joined reporters covering an insurrection of dervishes in Egypt (which ultimately led to the novel *The Tragedy of the "Korosko")*. He put everything aside to serve for several months as a doctor during the Boer Wars, much of it in a field hospital rife with enteric fever. He traveled to the front to research his history of World War I.

During all these campaigns, many of which are briefly recounted in the autobiographical *Memories and Adventures*, Conan Doyle speaks with unreserved admiration for the common English soldier and sailor and, in his view, their nearly always wise and valiant commanders. He never seems to have imagined that the British Empire could be seriously wrong, that the English presence in Egypt might be colonialist and oppressive to the indigenous people, that the Boers had a case, that the so-called Great War might be an unmitigated disaster and horror. Even in his later life, he continued to view himself as a selfless, knightly crusader—by then in the noble cause of Spiritualism.

Today, we tend to be leery of these old-fashioned ideals. Ardent patriotism can readily sink into unthinking jingoism. As it happens, glorification of the military occasionally leads even Conan Doyle to utter, approvingly, such barbaric statements as "Wonderful is the atmosphere of war. When the millennium comes the world will gain much, but it will lose its greatest thrill." (That sounds like Lord John Roxton, of *The Lost World,* at his most bloodthirsty.) He argues, too, that English boxing promoted a "combative spirit and aggressive quickness," which during the Great War "helped especially in bayonet work." Yet as a medical man, Conan Doyle must have known what bayonet work did to a human body.

At heart, though, Arthur Conan Doyle's soldierly character was more courtly than militaristic. From all the testimony, the man truly comported himself as a "parfit gentil knyght," to use Chaucer's phrase. Consider: In his late thirties this already married author met and fell in love with the strikingly beautiful Jean Leckie, age 23, and she with him. Louise, Conan Doyle's wife, was suffering from pulmonary disease and was essentially an invalid; the couple had probably given up all sexual relations. So, did this infatuated, vigorous man arrange to meet the woman of his dreams for nights of illicit love at the Victorian equivalent of Motel 6? It's certainly possible. Yet the most intense biographical research has failed to turn up any serious evidence of hanky-panky. Conan Doyle did spend time with Miss Leckie, but always in the presence of chaperones, among them his own mother. He continued to treat Touie, as he called his wife, with the utmost kindness, and never ceased to care for her. In the end, the writer and his beloved Jean waited ten years until Touie was dead, then waited another year until the proper period of mourning had elapsed, before they finally married. Conan Doyle, one feels, couldn't have brought himself to act in any other way. I'm not so sure about Jean.

Yet such iron devotion to duty shouldn't imply that Conan Doyle was a stick in the mud. The writer fully appreciated the good things in life. In 1883, for instance, young Arthur attended a ball where he got "as drunk as an owl" and proposed to half the women in the room, even those who were already married.

> I got one letter next day signed "Ruby" and saying the writer had said "yes" when she meant "no"—but who the deuce she was or what she had said "yes" about I can't conceive.

Years later and many pounds heavier, Conan Doyle remained a gregarious, clubbable man. He liked cigars, his pipe, and good wine, especially burgundy, employed as many as eight servants, and, to go by his photographs, routinely dressed with elegance and care. It's clear, however, that the Jesuit training at Stonyhurst College left Conan Doyle—even when he had rejected Catholicism—convinced that one should live a life of high principle. Writing, too, should serve noble ends. "The best literary work," he told the magazine *Tit-Bits* in 1910,

> is that which leaves the reader better for having read it. Now nobody can possibly be the better—in the high sense in which I mean it— for reading Sherlock Holmes, although he may have passed a pleasant hour in doing so. It was not to my mind high work, and no detective

work ever can be, apart from the fact that all work dealing with criminal matters is a cheap way of rousing the interest of the reader.

Instead of light fiction, Conan Doyle always recommended that his friends and family take up serious works, with pencil in hand:

> Read solid books, history, biography and travel—and above all take notes on what you read. Reading without note taking is as senseless as eating without digesting. It is easy to condense into a single page all that you really want to remember out of a big book, and there you have it for reference for ever. When you have done that systematically, for five years, you will be surprised at the extraordinary amount of available information which you can turn upon any subject, all at the cost of very little trouble.

He himself built up an extensive archive of letters, papers, clippings, and memoranda. One early biographer counted sixty scrapbooks alone.

Given Conan Doyle's character and background, it's no surprise that a combative spirit animates his abundant and varied journalism. In pamphlets, tracts, and letters to newspapers, he writes with an often angry purpose—to accuse, to exhort, to defend, to right wrongs. He attacks journalistic improprieties, proudly serves as the president of the Divorce Law Reform Union, argues for the adoption of body armor for soldiers, warns against the imminent threat of submarine warfare, advocates life-preserving "neck collars" for sailors, envisions the benefits of a Channel tunnel, and promotes the cause of Spiritualism. To give just one example: In a stirring letter to *The Times*, he condemns the Belgian atrocities in the Congo with savage, Swiftian indignation:

Sir,—We live in the presence of the greatest crime which has ever been committed in the history of the world, and yet we who not only could stop it but are bound by our sworn oath to stop it do nothing. The thing has been going on for 20 years. What are we waiting for? Our guilt of national acquiescence is only second to that of the gang of cosmopolitan scoundrels who have been actively concerned in turning all Central Africa into a huge slave State, with such attendant horrors as even the dark story of the slave trade has never shown. . . .

Periodically, in both senses of the word, this Lancelot gallops to the rescue of the insulted and injured, the downtrodden or abused. For instance, a young lawyer named George Edalji, an Englishman of Parsee extraction, was convicted of mutilating horses and cattle. It was a very strange affair, one combining obvious racial animosity, vicious practical jokes, and considerable police prejudice. When he learned of the case, Conan Doyle suspected that a serious wrong had occurred and so launched a scrupulous investigation of his own, until at last he felt that "it was an insult to my intelligence to hold out any longer against the certainty that there had been an inconceivable miscarriage of justice."

His articles about the case, later published as a small book, helped exonerate Edalji in the eyes of the public, even if Conan Doyle grew rightly disgusted by the ignoble failure of the judiciary to admit its errors. In 2005 Julian Barnes's *Arthur & George* undertook to reexamine and interpret this episode in Conan Doyle's life. This excellent if somewhat sober novel portrays two men victimized by their own highest ideals—Edalji by his belief in English justice, Conan Doyle by his reverence for the principles of honor and duty. As Barnes grimly concludes, Arthur loved his wife "as best a man can, given that he did not love her." In the year between Touie's death and marriage to Jean, the Edalji case galvanized him into needful, restorative action. Later, Conan Doyle would undertake a similar campaign to overthrow the murder conviction of Oscar Slater, accused of killing a rich woman for her jewelry. *The Case of Oscar Slater* (1912) has been called, by Jacques Barzun, "a masterpiece of analysis, reasoning, and exposition. It is moreover as good a story as any of the Holmes adventures."

Another masterpiece, albeit of quite a different character, is *Through the Magic Door*, Conan Doyle's celebration of his favorite authors. Directed mainly at young people, these essays may be blatantly didactic, yet one feels no qualms about paying heed to such impassioned lecturing and inspired quotation. In no sense a literary theorist or scholar, Conan Doyle emerges as that old-fashioned and oft-derided thing, a bookman. He speaks of the writers that have shaped his taste and character, and he tries to persuade his readers to appreciate their merits. His pieces—like the 1930s and '40s book columns of the eminent Sherlockians Vincent Starrett and Christopher Morley—resemble good talk more than they do *explication de texte*.

In the opening pages of *Through the Magic Door* Conan Doyle invites the reader to pass into his library. He then points out his serried rows of books, likening them to soldiers at attention. Here, he says, "you have left all that is vulgar and all that is sordid behind you. There stand your noble, silent comrades, waiting in their ranks." For Conan Doyle, "each cover of a true book enfolds the concentrated essence of a man." Through them, he says, "the dead man's wisdom and the dead man's example give us guidance and strength in the living of our own strenuous days." Indeed, he adds, "that is one of the things which human society has not yet understood— the value of a noble, inspiriting text."

To Sir Arthur Conan Doyle what matters most in literature isn't aesthetic perfection: What counts is that books be thrilling lessons in heroism, sacrifice, and virtuous action. In every case, what he responds to is the grand romantic gesture, the evidence of greatheartedness. Of one Walter Scott novel, he remarks, "Do you remember when the reckless Sergeant of Dragoons stands at last before the grim Puritan, upon whose head a price has been set: 'A thousand marks or a bed of heather!' says he, as he draws. The Puritan draws also: 'The Sword of the Lord and of Gideon,' says he." Conan Doyle adds, "No verbiage there! But the very spirit of either man and of either party, in the few stern words, which haunt your mind."

This notion of the author as a purveyor of Plutarchan values persists through all the chapters of *Through the Magic Door*. What is any given writer like as a man or woman? What examples and lessons does he or she pass on to humanity? "You can forgive old Pepys a good deal of his philandering," our amiable guide writes, "when you remember that he was the only official of the Navy Office who stuck to his post during the worst days of the Plague. He may have been— indeed, he assuredly was—a coward, but the coward who has sense of duty enough to overcome his cowardice is the most truly brave of mankind." On the flip side, Conan Doyle grows almost overheated about Henry Fielding: "Tom Jones was no more fit to touch the hem of Sophia's dress than Captain Booth was to be the mate of Amelia. Never once has Fielding drawn a gentleman, save perhaps Squire Allworthy. . . . Where, in his heroes, is there one touch of distinction, of spirituality, of nobility?"

Ultimately a man simply needs to do the right thing, stay true to the code of a gentleman, be a *mensch.* Those barefisted Regency boxers—Conan Doyle has a chapter about their memoirs—didn't just possess hearts of oak, they were oaks themselves, models of unflinching endurance.

> That is one of the weaknesses of modern life. We complain too much. We are not ashamed of complaining. Time was when it was otherwise . . . 'You look cold, sir,' said an English sympathizer to a French émigré. The fallen noble drew himself up in his threadbare coat. 'Sir,' said he, 'a gentleman is never cold.' One's consideration for others as well as one's own self-suppression, and also the concealment of pain are two of the old *noblesse oblige* characteristics which are now little more than a tradition.

Given such ideals, Conan Doyle would naturally create the self-sacrificing Sherlock Holmes, whom Watson describes in "The Final Problem"— his words echoing the description of Socrates in Plato's *Phaedo*—as "the best and wisest man I have ever known."

Of course, Conan Doyle did recognize that stories needed to be thrilling, amusing, or witty, else nobody would read them. He was, after all, the most successful professional writer of his time. So *Through the Magic Door* also offers particularly knowledgeable reflections on the art of narrative. Great short stories, we are told, are much rarer than great novels. They need "strength, novelty, compactness, intensity of interest, a single vivid impression upon the mind." Just so, "the supreme original short story writer of all time" was Edgar Allan Poe, whose "brain was like a seed-pod full of seeds which flew carelessly around, and from which have sprung nearly all our modern types of story."

What short fiction did Conan Doyle himself particularly admire? Here, and elsewhere, he mentions the following as personal favorites: Poe's "The Gold Bug" and "The Murders in the Rue Morgue," Bret Harte's "The Luck of Roaring Camp" and "Tennessee's Partner," Robert Louis Stevenson's "Dr. Jekyll and Mr. Hyde" and "The Pavilion on the Links"—this last seems to have been his pick for possibly the finest story in the world. He enthusiastically recommends Kipling's "The Drums of the Fore and Aft" and "The Man Who Would Be King," as well as Bulwer-Lytton's "The Haunted and the Haunters," which he calls "the very best ghost story that I know." He also praises two other classic tales of terror, Maupassant's "The Horla" and Ambrose Bierce's "In the Midst of Life."

And what of the novel? For the author of such historical epics as *Micah Clarke* and *The Refugees*, the longer the better. Samuel Richardson's *Clarissa*, he admits, "may be a little wearisome at first, if you have been accustomed to a more hustling style with fireworks in every chapter"—that certainly describes our twenty-first-century fiction—"but gradually it creates an atmosphere in which you live, and you come to know these people, with their characters and their troubles, as you know no others of the dream-folk of fiction." Yes, *Clarissa* may be "three times as long as an ordinary book no doubt, but why grudge the time? What is the hurry? Surely it is better to read one masterpiece than three books which will leave no permanent impression on the mind."

Looking back over nineteenth-century British novels, Conan Doyle points to a trio of masterpieces: Thackeray's *Vanity Fair*, Charles Reade's *The Cloister and the Hearth*—he ranks it with Tolstoy's *War and Peace*—and George Meredith's *The Ordeal of Richard Feverel*. He then goes on to commend George Borrow's autobiographical *Lavengro* and its author's other works—they show "heart." In American literature, besides the writers already mentioned, he admires Washington Irving—"no man wrote fresher English with a purer style"—

and singles out *The Conquest of Granada* for its portraits of gracious knights among both the Saracens and Christians. We also know—from an interview—that he regarded Hawthorne's *The Scarlet Letter* as "the greatest novel yet written by an American."

While I've enjoyed all of the short stories that Conan Doyle recommends, I confess that among these longer works—at least those just mentioned—I've only read the Hawthorne and the Thackeray. Could the others be just as good or nearly so? I have gone out and bought copies of them all. A few years back, Conan Doyle did steer me to Macaulay's collected essays—one of the key books of his youth—and these were just as he said: masterpieces of historical narrative and models of English prose. At the very least, then, *Through the Magic Door* is an ingratiating guide to neglected works of literature and history.

Arthur Conan Doyle once recalled a friend saying, in two dramatic understatements, "that my letters were very vivid and surely I could write things to sell." Much the same ingratiating ease and charm of *Through the Magic Door* can be found throughout *Arthur Conan Doyle: A Life in Letters*, edited by Jon Lellenberg, Daniel Stashower, and Charles Foley. Even as a schoolboy writing home to his mother, Conan Doyle reveals his instinctive grasp for narrative pace and understated comedy: "We have had a great commotion here lately, from the fact that our third prefect has gone stark staring mad. . . . They say that in his delirium he mentioned my name several times."

Many of the great writer's reprinted lectures and talks make for equally good reading. Consider "The Romance of Medicine," an address that might be easily mistaken for one of the stirring medico-humanist essays of William Osler. "The moral training to keep a confidence inviolate, to act promptly on a sudden call, to keep your head in critical moments, to be kind and yet strong—where can you, outside medicine, get such a training as that?" In sum, "To the man who has mastered *Gray's Anatomy*, life holds no further terrors."

That last sentence again exhibits Conan Doyle's dry and often subtly oblique humor. In a toast to "The Immortal Memory" of Robert Burns, he noted that Burns's love poems are undeniably heartfelt and melodious, but "we might wish, perhaps, that there was less variety in the names which we find in them." During a particularly delightful speech given before the Prince of Wales and 400 others—Conan Doyle claims it was the most successful of his career—he took up, with tongue in cheek, the illnesses of convenience regularly encountered in modern novels:

> We only recognize in my calling, the writing of fiction, certain diseases; the others are of no use to us. . . . There is, of course, phthisis. I do not know how we should get on with our heroines without it. We sometimes call it a decline, sometimes we call it a wilting away. This is most useful to us, and it ends usually in a complete cure in the second last chapter. The treatment, of course, consists in the bringing back of that great and good man who has been so cruelly misunderstood in Chapter IV. The symptoms of this disease are acute but variable. The most prominent one is extreme wasting, coupled with an almost ethereal beauty.

To some modern tastes, Conan Doyle's autobiographical *Memories and Adventures* is slightly too much a model of reserve and discretion, despite its author having led "a life which, for variety and romance, could, I think, hardly be exceeded." Youthful adventures at sea, early years as a doctor, the slow discovery of a literary vocation, friendships with the famous writers of his generation—all these are fascinatingly recalled. Conan Doyle relates, for example, some of the puns and ripostes of his brother-in-law E. V. Hornung, the creator of Raffles, the gentleman-thief. (The first collection of Raffles stories, *The Amateur Cracksman*, was dedicated "To ACD—this form of flattery.") When someone claimed to have run a hundred-yard dash in under ten seconds, Hornung immediately replied: "It is a sprinter's error." Capping his explanation of why he could not abide golf, Hornung asserted that it was "unsportsmanlike to hit a sitting ball."

While E. V. Hornung's wordplay was obviously amusing, Oscar Wilde possessed a deeper wit, his best epigrams incorporating shrewd observations about life: "I like persons better than principles, and I like persons with no principles better than anything else in the world." In one the most delightful interludes in the history of serendipity, two bright young literary men were once invited to dinner at the Langham Hotel by the editor of *Lippincott's Magazine*. That evening in 1889 J. M. Stoddart signed up both of them to write novels. The result? A. Conan Doyle's *The Sign of the Four* and Oscar Wilde's *The Picture of Dorian Gray*.

Conan Doyle seems never to have forgotten that evening nor the doomed aesthete. In the pages of *Memories and Adventures* he recalls Wilde at his youthful best:

He had a curious precision of statement, a delicate flavour of humour, and a trick of small gestures to illustrate his meaning, which were peculiar to himself. The effect cannot be reproduced, but I remember how in discussing the wars of the future he said: "A chemist on each side will approach the frontier with a bottle"—his upraised hand and precise face conjuring up a vivid and grotesque picture.

His anecdotes, too, were happy and curious. We were discussing the cynical maxim that the good fortune of our friends made us discontented. "The devil," said Wilde, "was once crossing the Libyan Desert, and he came upon a spot where a number of small fiends were tormenting a holy hermit. The sainted man easily shook off their evil suggestions. The devil watched their failure and then he stepped forward to give them a lesson. 'What you do is too crude,' said he. 'Permit me for one moment.' With that he whispered to the holy man, 'Your brother has just been made Bishop of Alexandria.' A scowl of malignant jealousy at once clouded the serene face of the hermit. 'That,' said the devil to his imps, 'is the sort of thing which I should recommend.' "

Naturally, *Memories and Adventures* can hardly avoid some scattered comments—all too few—about the hero of "A Tangled Skein," the formidable Sherringford Holmes (or Hope) and his friend Ormond Sacker. For so *A Study in Scarlet* might have been called, and so its heroes were almost named. "The difficulty of the Holmes work," Conan Doyle frankly confesses, "was that every story really needed as clear-cut and original a plot as a longish book would do. One cannot without effort spin plots at such a rate. They are apt to thin or to break." So he resolved never to write about Holmes "without a worthy plot and without a problem which interested my own mind, for that is the first requisite before you can interest any one else."

"People," he continues,

have often asked me whether I knew the end of a Holmes story before I started it. Of course I do. One could not possibly steer a course if one did not know one's destination. The first thing is to get your idea. Having got that key idea one's next task is to conceal it and lay emphasis upon everything which can make for a different explanation. Holmes, however, can see all the fallacies of the alternatives, and arrives more or less dramatically at the true solution by steps which he can describe and justify. He shows his powers by . . . clever little deductions, which often have nothing to do with the matter in hand, but impress the reader with a general sense of power. The same effect is gained by his offhand allusion to other cases. Heaven knows how many titles I have thrown about in a casual way, and how many readers have begged me to satisfy their curiosity as to "Rigoletto and His Abominable Wife," "The Adventure of the Tired Captain," or "The Curious Experience of the Patterson Family in the Island of Uffa." Once or twice, as in "The Adventure of the Second Stain," which in my judgment is one of the neatest of the stories, I did actually use the title years before I wrote a story to correspond.

Such comments disclose how thoughtfully Conan Doyle approached his writing, even that which he would sometimes later dismiss or misjudge. Holmes's character, he tells us, "admits no light or shade. He is a calculating machine, and anything you add to that simply weakens the effect." That's only true of the early stories, while the detective's myriad eccentricities and crotchets are actually what endear him to readers. And while one can hardly dispute that a consulting detective's adventures "must depend upon the romance and compact handling of the plots," we mainly return to Baker Street for the comforting talk and exhilarating company of Holmes and Watson.

Whenever Conan Doyle discusses the technique of the mystery, he sounds very much the careful student of Poe's "Philosophy of Composition," that blueprint for tight verbal construction and unity of effect. But he also reminds the novice to build up his vocabulary, to adopt a style that doesn't draw undue attention to itself, to be natural. Above all, he argues that good writing should follow three rules: "The first requisite is to be intelligible. The second is to be interesting. The third is to be clever."

Conan Doyle himself was an extremely fast writer, yet his penmanship always remained clear and easy to read: The surviving holographs for his stories seldom reveal many second thoughts or revisions. Quite amazingly, on the first day that he moved into his new ophthalmologic office in London—April 1 or 2, 1891—he set to work on "A

Scandal in Bohemia" and the first set of Sherlock Holmes stories. "His pocket diary," adds the historian Owen Dudley Edwards, "shows the speed at which the stories were written. The first was dispatched to . . . his literary agent, on 3 April. On 10 April 'A Case of Identity' was finished. On 20 April, 'The Red-Headed League' was sent off, and 'The Boscombe Valley Mystery' followed on 27 April." Bear in mind that on average the Sherlock Holmes stories run to roughly 8,000 words—and that at least two of these four stories, produced in less than a month, are among the finest in all the canon.

Conan Doyle, moreover, could produce sentences steadily from morning to night. In a late essay on his working habits, he declared:

> As to my hours of work, when I am keen on a book I am prepared to work all day, with an hour or two of walk or siesta in the afternoon. As I grow older I lose some power of sustained effort, but I remember that I once did ten thousand words of *The Refugees* in twenty-four hours. . . . Twice I have written forty-thousand word pamphlets in a week, but in each case I was sustained by a burning indignation, which is the best driving power.

For useful comparison, the reader might note that this little book clocks in at about 45,000 words. It took much longer than a week to write.

"I Hear of Sherlock Everywhere"

After I returned from the road trip to Mexico during which I'd read *The Poison Belt*, summer was virtually over. At the end of August I started my freshman year at nearby Oberlin College, having resolutely decided to put away childish things, like adventure stories and comics and science fiction and Sherlock Holmes. It was time to buckle down. Yet the Great Detective was not so easily forgotten, as Conan Doyle himself quickly realized after he had supposedly sent Holmes and Professor Moriarty tumbling to their deaths at the Reichenbach Falls.

While I resolutely determined to transform myself from a Wild Ginger Man into a studious grind, come Friday night I'd always spend an hour in the dorm lounge watching *Star Trek*. As others have remarked, Mr. Spock—that half-human, half-Vulcan calculating machine—is clearly derived from Holmes with, it seemed to me, a touch or two of the detective's elder brother Mycroft.

Mycroft only appears briefly in the canon (chiefly in "The Greek Interpreter" and "The Bruce-Partington Plans"), but is nonetheless quite unforgettable. Sherlock himself regards his brother as his superior in "observation and deduction."

Sedentary and precise in his routines—"Mycroft has his rails and he runs on them"—this supposed minor bureaucrat actually functions as "the central exchange, the clearing-house" for all government intelligence. "In that great brain of his everything is pigeon-holed, and can be handed out in an instant." In essence, Mycroft is a human computer like Spock. With his sharp analytic intelligence, impressive bulk, and insistence on a regular schedule, he also closely resembles Rex Stout's gruff consulting detective Nero Wolfe. Years later, I would learn that some Sherlockian scholars believe that Wolfe's mother was Irene Adler and his father either Sherlock or Mycroft.

One day late in the fall term of my freshman year, I discovered that one of my new friends, Roger Phelps, had stayed up all night rereading Sherlock Holmes stories. Being down in the dumps, he had burrowed back into them for comfort and renewal. When I stopped by his room in Burton Hall, we proceeded to share favorite passages from his worn Doubleday edition. On that typically bleak day in Oberlin, we naturally gravitated to those cases that evoked the cozy snugness of 221B—for instance, "The Five Orange Pips," which opens this way:

> It was in the latter days of September, and the equinoctial gales had set in with exceptional violence. All day the wind had screamed and the rain had beaten against the windows . . . . Sherlock Holmes sat moodily at one side of the fireplace cross-indexing his records of crime, while I at the other was deep in one of Clark Russell's fine sea stories, until the howl of the gale from without seemed to blend with the text, and the splash of the rain to lengthen out into the long swash of sea waves. . . .
>
>   "Why," said I, glancing up at my companion, "that was surely the bell. Who could come to-night?"

And soon the game is afoot.

Like all Sherlockians, Roger and I would speculate about those many unrecorded cases to which Watson regularly alludes and for which "the world is not yet prepared," the most famous being that of the Giant Rat of Sumatra. In "The

Five Orange Pips," itself a strikingly evocative title, Watson is especially tantalizing:

> The year '87 furnished us with a long series of cases of greater or less interest, of which I retain the records. Among my headings under this one twelve months, I find an account of the adventure of the Paradol Chamber, of the Amateur Mendicant Society, who held a luxurious club in the lower vault of a furniture warehouse, of the facts connected with the loss of the British barque *Sophy Anderson*, of the singular adventures of the Grice Pattersons in the island of Uffa, and finally the Camberwell poisoning case. . . . But none of them present such singular features as the strange train of circumstances which I have now taken up my pen to describe.

See what I mean? As Holmes would say, the merest mention of those unpublished exploits sets the imagination afire. What were "the colossal schemes" of the Baron Maupertuis? What are the facts in "the repulsive story of the red leech and the terrible death of Crosby, the banker"? Who wouldn't wish to hear more of "Wilson, the notorious canary trainer" and "Huret, the boulevard assassin"? Most tantalizing of all is "the whole story of the politician, the lighthouse and the trained cormorant," which Watson threatens to reveal to the public unless certain "outrages" and attempts to destroy his papers immediately cease.

As a potential English major, I was naturally enrolled in an array of literature classes, for which I produced essays and term papers based on the close-reading techniques of the New Criticism. Not that these techniques seemed particularly new to me. Weren't they merely Holmes's usual *modus operandi* applied to poems and stories? One simply needed to pay close attention to the words and look carefully at anything particularly odd or distinctive. "Singularity," as the Master often observed, "is almost invariably a clue." Holmes's success, as he told Watson more than once, lay in "the observance of trifles." I soon realized that Sherlock Holmes "read" a person or crime in the way a critic such as William Empson read poetry. Moreover, both these readers—Empson with his own brash self-confidence—liked to show off and amaze. As Holmes says, "the quick inference, the subtle trap, the clever forecast of coming events, the triumphant vindication of bold theories—are these not the pride and the justification of our life's work?"

During my freshman year I also grew besotted with T. S. Eliot, and boldly decided to read everything from the early essays in *The Sacred Wood* to the later verse-dramas. At some point I discovered that Eliot revered the Sherlock Holmes stories. At a party one evening, some friends asked him to name his favorite passage of English prose, and the great poet answered by virtually performing the following exchange:

"Well," cried Boss McGinty at last, "is he here? Is Birdy Edwards here?"

"Yes," McMurdo answered slowly. "Birdy Edwards is here. I am Birdy Edwards."

Was Eliot joking with his audience by choosing this climactic passage from *The Valley of Fear*? At least a little, I suspect. Nonetheless, Eliot reportedly reread the Holmes canon every couple of years, was an honorary member of the Trained Cormorants of Los Angeles, and looked—as Vincent Starrett observed—more like the Great Detective than many of the actors who played him.

Moreover, Eliot wrote at length about Holmes in the *Criterion*, modeled "Macavity, the Mystery Cat," aka the Hidden Paw, after that other Napoleon of Crime, Professor James Moriarty, and in

"East Coker" quite pointedly evoked the atmosphere of *The Hound of the Baskervilles* by alluding to the novel's ominous Grimpen Mire: "in a dark wood, in a bramble / On the edge of a grimpen, where is no secure foothold." While Eliot famously insisted that great poets steal, I was nonetheless taken aback when I first came across this striking exchange between Thomas Becket and a diabolical Tempter in *Murder in the Cathedral*:

> THOMAS: Who shall have it?
> TEMPTER: He who will come.
> THOMAS: What shall be the month?
> TEMPTER: The last from the first.
> THOMAS: What shall we give for it?
> TEMPTER: Pretence of priestly power.
> THOMAS: Why should we give it?
> TEMPTER: For the power and the glory.

In "The Musgrave Ritual"—one of Holmes's earliest cases—an aristocratic family preserves for centuries a queer litany, which, of course, provides the key to a riddle and the solution to a strange disappearance:

> "Whose was it?"
> "His who is gone."

"Who shall have it?"

"He who will come."

("What was the month?"

"The sixth from the first.") . . . .

"What shall we give for it?"

"All that is ours."

"Why should we give it?"

"For the sake of the trust."

Wherever I turned, it seemed that I chanced upon Sherlockian allusions and echoes. When I spent part of a summer with Boswell's *Life of Samuel Johnson* I recognized that the conversational interplay between the Great Cham and his biographer prefigured the back-and-forth at 221B Baker Street. (Lillian de la Torre ran with this idea in *Dr. Sam: Johnson, Detector.*) During one Christmas break I picked up *The Wind in the Willows* and suddenly noticed that Rat clamps on a deerstalker before he goes searching for Mole in the Wild Wood. The two friends are then lost together in a snowstorm, when Mole trips over some unseen object:

"It's a very clear cut," said the Rat, examining it again attentively. "That was never done by a branch or a stump. Looks as if it was made by a sharp edge of something in metal. Funny!"

He pondered awhile, and examined the humps and slopes that surrounded them.

The pair dig through the snow and uncover a doorscraper. Mole, like Watson, fails to perceive its significance. "But don't you see what it *means*— you dull witted animal!" It means, of course, that there's a door nearby, in this case, Badger's door. At which point, Watson, I mean Mole, is finally impressed by his friend's deductive reasoning: "I've read about that sort of thing in books, but I've never come across it before in real life."

I spent most of my twenties in graduate school at Cornell University, taking courses in medieval studies and European romanticism, and gradually working toward a Ph.D. in comparative literature. Ambitious as only youth can be, I aspired to know everything about fiction and poetry, art, music, philosophy, and history. As Holmes once observed, "All knowledge comes useful to the detective"—and to the would-be teacher of literature as well. In the early days of their association, Watson had admittedly been appalled to hear that his flatmate was unaware that the earth revolves around the sun. However, most students of the canon now agree that Holmes was either playing games with Watson or simply being cautious about revealing too much about himself to his new associate.

Later on we discover that this violinist, forensic scientist, amateur boxer, and gifted actor can quote not only the details of every horrid crime of the century but also Hafiz, Petrarch, and Goethe. He's not only written about the influence of various trades upon the shape of the hand, and distinguished among 140 different kinds of tobacco ash, but also contributed articles to scholarly journals on the dating of documents and the motets of Lassus. He's a frequent concertgoer and something of a connoisseur of wine. When engaged on a case he will frequently work himself up to a state of "nervous exaltation," but overall he views existence with considerable pessimism: "Is not all life pathetic and futile? . . . We reach. We grasp. And what is left in our hands at the end? A shadow. Or worse than a shadow—misery."

Acquiring knowledge and exercising the intellect are ways of driving off the spleen. On one particularly brilliant evening, Watson tells us, he heard this polymath speak "on a quick succession of subjects—on miracle plays, on medieval pottery, on Stradivarius violins, on the Buddhism of Ceylon, and on the warships of the future, handling each as though he had made a special study of it."

At Cornell, my reading and coursework in nineteenth-century fiction gradually uncovered some of the sources for that foggy gaslit London through which the Baker Street duo hurry when the game is afoot. Balzac, Hugo, Dickens, and Eugène Sue revealed that beneath the bustling modern city there existed dark criminal labyrinths, urban jungles, and even Arabian Nights–like realms of opulence and mystery. In Hugo's *Notre Dame de Paris*, for instance, the poet Pierre Gringoire plunges into a nightmarish maze of alleyways that gradually lead downward into the hall of the Gypsy king, who rules, Moriarty-like, over the city's underclass.

Conan Doyle always insisted that Holmes took shape from memories of the analytic Joseph Bell reinforced by the brilliant example of Edgar Allan Poe's Auguste Dupin, who solves "The Murders in the Rue Morgue." I suspect that Fenimore Cooper's Mohican trackers also played a part: When examining the scene of a crime, Holmes—whose "countenance" is likened to that of a "Red Indian" in "The Naval Treaty"— frequently drops to the ground to search out unnoticed signs and clues, whether a bent twig or a heel print. Robert

Louis Stevenson—in some ways Poe's Scottish cousin—provides yet another partial inspiration. The first story in *New Arabian Nights*, "The Young Man with the Cream Tarts," opens when the London fog rolls in, and out of the darkness emerge two figures. One is tall, eccentric in his habits, in search of mysteries and puzzles; the other is his brave and loyal companion, evidently a military man. Sound familiar?

In the course of their exploits Prince Florizel and Colonel Geraldine fearlessly penetrate the inner sanctum of the Suicide Club, confront more than one master criminal, and eventually solve the theft of the accursed Rajah's Diamond. Like a set of *matryoshka* dolls, conspiracies turn out to be embedded within other conspiracies, while the various sinister characters and seemingly nonsensical incidents often recall those that were later to confront Holmes. Why, for instance, should a young man be forced to eat, or give strangers to eat, dozens of cream tarts? Why has a mysterious gentleman rented a grand house for one night and then paid hansom cabs to pick up casual passersby and bring them to his party? Why should a pretty girl suddenly say to her admirer, "Whatever happens, do not return to this house; hurry fast until you reach the lighted and populous quarters of the city; even there be upon your guard. You are in a greater danger than you fancy"? This, surely, is the same London as that of "The Red-Headed League," *The Sign of the Four,* and "The Man with the Twisted Lip." Little wonder that Stevenson's executor hoped, unsuccessfully, that Conan Doyle would complete the unfinished *St. Ives.*

I moved to Washington, D.C., to finish my dissertation (on the French writer Stendhal). There I initially taught part-time at American University and George Mason University, and later picked up work as a translator, freelance editor, and, *mirabile dictu,* technical writer for a computer company. Only at the age of 29 did I begin to write about books for the *Washington Post.* After publishing a dozen reviews, I was offered a job as an assistant editor in *Book World.* I took it. After all, I could see that computers were going nowhere. Clearly my deductive skills more closely resembled those of Inspector Lestrade than those of Sherlock Holmes.

In Washington I soon began building a personal library. Over the years I had admired and envied the book collections of my various professors: leather-bound rows of classics, beautiful editions of modern firsts, expensive scholarly tomes, the complete works of favorite writers. Little did I know then that book collecting is less about acquiring books than about finding the shelf space to store them. Still, in those halcyon days before the Internet took away all the romance from booking, I regularly wandered around the capital in search of treasures, and always made sure to be near the front of the line at the annual Brandeis, State Department, Goodwill, and Stone Ridge book sales.

As a novice collector eager for guidance, I particularly enjoyed reading booksellers' memoirs—and once again, I began to hear of Sherlock everywhere. In David A. Randall's *Dukedom Large Enough* I learned that the author, Scribner's longtime rare book expert and the first director of Indiana's Lilly Library, had been a prominent member of The Baker Street Irregulars. John Carter, author of the high-spirited *ABC of Book Collecting*, was also known for a ground-breaking monograph on collecting detective fiction, an essay in which Holmes's exploits featured prominently. Carter himself first gained fame as a bibliographical Sherlock, being the coauthor with Graham Pollard of the innocent-sounding *An Enquiry into the Nature of Certain Nineteenth-Century Pamphlets*, which proved that the leading book collector of his time, Sir Thomas Wise, was an out-and-out forger.

To this day I would agree with Vincent Starrett that "when we are collecting books, we are collecting happiness." Starrett, a Chicago-based newspaper columnist, wrote not only *Bookman's Holiday* and *Born in a Bookshop*, but also the seminal *Private Life of Sherlock Holmes* (1933). His long-running column "Books Alive" provided a smorgasbord of publishing news and mini-essays about every aspect of the literary life, but also frequently reported on the latest activities of The Baker Street Irregulars. When Starrett needed to dispose of his own library of rarities, he naturally sold it to David Randall.

My own collecting—at least back then—more closely resembled that of Christopher Morley, this country's other great champion of Sherlockian studies (and Starrett's good friend). Morley concluded an expanded version of "In Memoriam," his introduction to *The Complete Sherlock Holmes*, with a prose aria about the Conan Doyle treasures on his own shelves:

> As with all esteemed authors, there is too much talk of first editions and fine copies and

not nearly enough about the chance examples and shabby second-hand culls that we more frequently encounter. Does no one else take pleasure in phony copies, piracies, wretched reprints jobbed off for mail-order sets and department store trading? What an oddly miscellaneous spectacle is the collection of any average Doyle enthusiast. . . . I have some genuine firsts among them, but not less prized are the queer and abominable copies picked up from time to time at hazard. My American edition of the *Stark Munro Letters* (Appleton '95) has the rubber stamp of the Y.M.C.A. Library, Montreal. *Beyond the City*, vilely impressed on brittle yellowing paper, was sponsored by F. Tennyson Nicely, 1894. *A Study in Scarlet* is one of a set imprinted W.R. Caldwell and Co. *The Firm of Girdlestone* carries the name of Siegel Cooper & Co., New York and Chicago. Most mysterious of the lot is *A Case of Identity and Other Stories*, from The Optimus Printing Company, 45–51 Rose Street, New York, down by the Brooklyn Bridge. Next after Oscar Wilde, poor old Conan Doyle must have been utilized by more will-o'-the-wisp publishers than any other modern writer.

Thus it was in a Goodwill thrift shop that I unearthed a jacketed first edition of Edgar W. Smith's *Profile by Gaslight*, an anthology of writings "about the private life of Sherlock Holmes," first published in 1944. More than any other, Smith, an executive for General Motors, brought order and system to The Baker Street Irregulars, such that the society's survival to the present day is largely due to his genius and hard work. Among the essays in this groundbreaking collection are some of the most famous in the annals of Sherlockiana. Dorothy L. Sayers, exercising an ingenuity worthy of her own Lord Peter Wimsey, determined the middle name of John H. Watson (answer: Hamish). Fletcher Pratt, whose *Secret and Urgent: The Story of Codes and Ciphers* I had read as a boy, analyzed "The Secret Message of the Dancing Men." "The Significance of the Second Stain" was written by Felix Morley, at one time the editor of my own newspaper, the *Washington Post*. He was also Christopher Morley's brother. (Frank, the third Morley brother, worked at Faber and Faber in London, at one time sharing an office there with his friend T. S. Eliot.)

Still, the most famous, indeed notorious, contribution to the book was that of Rex Stout, in which the creator of Nero Wolfe determined to his own satisfaction that "Watson was a Woman." Years later in *Ms. Holmes of Baker Street* Alan Bradley and William Sarjeant would argue, with comparable finesse, that it was actually Holmes who was the woman. ("You know my methods in such cases, Watson. I put myself in the *man's* place.") Inevitably, yet another investigator, Alastair Martin, attempted to prove that Professor Moriarty was female—and that Holmes married her during the great hiatus. No one, so far as I am aware, has yet questioned Mycroft's sex— though he does resemble Queen Victoria in drag. Something, perhaps, to look into.

After reading *Profile by Gaslight*, I immediately decided that Sherlockian scholarship was a very strange business and probably not for me. So I sold the book for ten or twenty dollars through a tiny ad in *Antiquarian Bookman*, the monthly magazine of the used book trade. Twenty years later I would have to go out and buy another copy—and have to settle for a second printing.

In the 1980s I began to travel to London with some regularity, often staying in Camden Town with my friends John and Judith Clute. In those days John was still actively building one of the most astonishing personal libraries of our time, the foundation of his critical and biographical work as coeditor and major writer of *The Encyclopedia of Science Fiction* and *The Encyclopedia of Fantasy*. On Saturday mornings he would generally bicycle or drive down to Farringdon Road, where George Jeffery held the last remaining license to sell books from barrows on the streets of London. When I was in town, John took me along.

People often imagine the book trade to be a genteel business, but it isn't at all: Runners—as the British call used-book scouts—are melancholy, sinewy men of indeterminate age, tough as rugby players, edgy as bike couriers. Come the end of the day or a sale, they will sip a Guinness, recall treasures lost and found, grow almost gregarious, but while the book-fit is on them, they are ruthless, predatory, insatiable. Through John, I met the legendary Martin Stone, then widely regarded as the best runner in England, heard about the notorious Driffield or Drif (author of *All the Second Hand and Antiquarian Bookshops in Britain*), and was introduced to Iain Sinclair, now known less for his expertise in beat literature than for his rococo prose style and such highly original novels as *White Chappell Scarlet Tracings*. That genre-bending thriller opens with a trio of scouts—clearly based on the author, Stone, and Driffield—invading a provincial bookshop and unearthing a *Beeton's* Christmas Annual for 1887. This is, of course, the most valuable magazine in the world, since it contains the first appearance of *A Study in Scarlet*. There are just 31 known copies, and only eleven are in decent shape. Today a fine *Beeton's* might easily go for a quarter of a million dollars.

I never had such luck. Still, on those frosty Saturday mornings George would whip off the canvas tarp covering his one-pounders and all the runners would grab books as fast as they could make out their titles. On one glorious occasion I did acquire the first two bound volumes of the *Strand Magazine*, the second containing "A Scandal in Bohemia" and the next five adventures of Sherlock Holmes. Once again, my then dormant passion for the Great Detective was starting to reawaken.

As a staffer at *Book World* I was able to follow my catholic, if sometimes peculiar, tastes in the titles I chose to review. I might commend a history of late antiquity one week, a new translation of Baudelaire the next, and a trio of Harlequin romances after that. When I read Daniel Pinkwater's *The Snarkout Boys and the Avocado of Death* (as well as its sequel *The Snarkout Boys and the Baconburg Horror*) I was tickled when the young heroes join forces with an eccentric investigator named Sigerson and his sidekick Dr. Ormond Sacker. Because of my medievalist background, I was a natural to review Umberto Eco's *The Name of the Rose,* and it didn't escape my notice that its Holmes-like detective was a tall aquiline monk named William of Baskerville.

In the mid-1980s my friend Bruce Cook— who, as Bruce Alexander, later wrote some excellent mysteries featuring the blind eighteenth-century jurist Sir John Fielding—asked me to review two Holmes pastiches for the *Detroit News.* Looking up the piece recently, I discovered that I was lukewarm about Michael Hardwick's *Sherlock Holmes and the Prisoner of the Devil* (in which the detective takes on the Dreyfus case) and only a little more enthusiastic about the H. F. Heard "Mr. Mycroft" classic *A Taste of Honey.* I suspect I'd feel differently about the latter now.

However, I lavished wholehearted praise on the handsome and compact nine volumes of *The Oxford Sherlock Holmes*, first published in 1993. Delineating its virtues in "Readings," my chatty bookman-like column for the *Post*, I drew especial attention to the superb introductions and annotations by the eminent Conan Doyle scholars Owen Dudley Edwards, Richard Lancelyn

Green, Christopher Roden, and W. W. Robson. The following year I then reviewed a much anticipated thriller called *Nevermore* by William Hjortsberg. It featured Harry Houdini and Sir Arthur Conan Doyle.

Hjortsberg's previous novel, *Falling Angel* (1978), ranks as a genuine cult classic. Cult is in fact the *mot juste*, since the mystery—about a private eye's search for a missing 1940s crooner—describes Harry Angel's descent into satanism, vodoun, and murderous ritual. In the more light-hearted *Nevermore*, Conan Doyle and Houdini merely pursue a serial killer who murders by the book, that book being *The Collected Works of Edgar Allan Poe.* Each gruesome death appears to be inspired by a Poe title—"The Murders in the Rue Morgue," "The Black Cat," "The Cask of Amontillado." Hjortsberg's thriller is set in 1923; Conan Doyle was by then a convinced spiritualist, and, in the course of the action, actually makes contact with the ghostly and rather depressed Poe. In the end there's poetic justice for the Poetic murderer. Hardly a significant book, it was nonetheless excellent Halloween fare.

Best of all, that same year I also wrote about *The Game Is Afoot: Parodies, Pastiches and Ponderings of Sherlock Holmes,* edited by Marvin

Kaye. Before then, I had had no full understanding of just how much an afterlife the great detective enjoyed in the fiction of other writers. (As of 2011, there are well over 7,000 known pastiches.) In Kaye's anthology, for instance, I first read Bret Harte's "The Stolen Cigar-Case," often called the most brilliant of all Sherlockian parodies. It opens: "I found Hemlock Jones in the old Brook Street lodgings, musing before the fire. With the freedom of an old friend I at once threw myself in my usual familiar attitude at his feet and gently caressed his boot." Kaye also included Vincent Starrett's "The Adventure of the Unique Hamlet," perhaps the best imitation Holmes adventure ever written; Jacques Barzun's speculations on how Holmes came to play the violin; and Poul Anderson's dazzling deductions about the "singular adventures of the Grice Pattersons in the Island of Uffa." That odd word "in" provides the key.

All in all, Sherlockian enthusiasts suddenly might be found anywhere. For a year or two I corresponded with the novelist Paul Horgan about our mutual fondness for the gossipy letters between publisher Rupert Hart-Davis and his old tutor George Lyttelton. After Horgan sent me a copy of his anthology *Maurice Baring Restored*, I began to seek out that neglected author's fiction and nonfiction. Thus it was that I discovered Baring's wildly funny "From the Diary of Sherlock Holmes":

> Baker Street, January 1.—Starting a diary in order to jot down a few useful incidents which will be of no use to Watson. Watson very often fails to see that an unsuccessful case is more interesting from a professional point of view than a successful one. He means well.

I also learned that nearly everyone's favorite comic genius was a longtime member of the fan club: "When I was starting out as a writer," P. G. Wodehouse once wrote, "Conan Doyle was my hero. Others might revere Hardy and Meredith. I was a Doyle man, and I still am." For proof one need only turn to the opening of his classic Adrian Mulliner story, "From a Detective's Notebook":

> Looking back over my years as a detective, I recall many problems the solutions of which made me modestly proud, but though all of them undoubtedly presented certain features of interest and tested my powers to the utmost, I can think of none of my feats of ratio-

cination which gave me more pleasure than the unmasking of the man Sherlock Holmes, now better known as the Fiend of Baker Street.

Wodehouse wrote only one Adrian Mulliner story, alas. But Robert L. Fish produced a series of short comic adventures nearly as good: *The Incredible Schlock Homes* and its sequels. These cases of Homes and Dr. Watney—full of puns and deliberately bad jokes—became my preferred bedtime reading for a happy month: During one case Watney exclaims that Homes in disguise is "fully a foot shorter!" and the detective replies, "Special shoes." On another memorable occasion, Homes confesses, "To my mind, Watney, sabotage—next to the pilfering of coal—is the dirtiest of all crimes!"

Given such abundance, I shouldn't have been surprised when I dropped by a D.C. art gallery and there on the wall hung what appeared to be Sidney Paget's illustration of Holmes and Moriarty grappling on a path high above the Reichenbach Falls. Only now a contemporary artist, Mark Tansey, had altered the image so that the cliffs were made of texts and the picture was deliciously retitled "Derrida queries de Man."

From my days at Cornell—home to the journal *Diacritics*—I already knew that contemporary literary theorists such as Jacques Derrida and Paul de Man found much to ponder in detective stories. Jacques Lacan demonstrated as much in his influential seminar on "The Purloined Letter," while Umberto Eco and Thomas A. Sebeok actually entitled a collection of semiotic essays, *The Sign of Three: Dupin, Holmes, Peirce*. I've long regretted not being able to buy the Tansey.

By this time, fascinated by the Sherlockianism of all these novelists and critics, I decided to dabble with deduction myself. So one Sunday my "Readings" page carried the following item:

> Recently, while skimming through a sale catalogue from Michael R. Thompson, Bookseller, I paused at an entry for deconstructionist philosopher Jacques Derrida's translation of a work by Edmund Husserl. Nothing to make the heart leap, you would think. But the catalogue went on to say, "First edition of Derrida's first book, presentation copy, inscribed to Susan Sontag." I went back and studied more carefully the bibliographical description, which ends with the devastating words, "A fine copy, uncut and unopened."

Derrida's book came out in 1962, and it seemed easy to imagine that Sontag received it at the time of publication, since she was living in Paris around then. But she was not yet famous—*Against Interpretation* appeared in 1966—and the more I pondered the entry, the more tantalizing it grew. Did young Sontag recognize young Derrida's genius? Were they friends? It didn't seem likely that she had bought the book and then asked him to sign it—in such a case, she would surely have cut the pages in order to read at least a little of its contents. Was it then a present from Derrida in recognition of Sontag's talents? And did her failure to read the book indicate her low regard for the Frenchman? In the most likely scenario, it would seem that Sontag had felt compelled to accept an inscribed copy of a work she didn't want. Which would suggest that she took it out of friendship or social obligation.

And yet since the book has only appeared on the market now, why would she have kept it all these years? As a sentimental memento? Of what? And would she have discarded it only recently because she had come to object to its author or his recent writings? Perhaps Derrida's defense of Paul de Man, the disgraced

Yale professor who authored some anti-Semitic writings in his youth, so enraged Sontag that she rid herself of this long-preserved and valuable possession? (The dealer is asking $1,500.) Holmes, thou shouldst be living at this hour!

Of course, one could simply call up Michael R. Thompson, Bookseller, and ask him how he acquired the volume and what the inscription says, but that would be far too easy. Instead I like to picture a sleazy left-wing cafe, Susan in a black turtleneck, Jacques looking almost collegiate in his navy pullover; in the background accordion music starts to play as Edith Piaf sings "*Non, je ne regrette rien.*" Smiling, the youthful philosopher writes a warm inscription in his new book and gives it to the *jolie Americaine.* Their hands touch. It is Paris, thinks Susan, "*Non, je ne regrette rien.*" She picks up her notebooks from the *papeterie* Joseph Gibert, the tattered copy of Kojève's study of Hegel. Together the couple walks away into the shimmering twilight, speaking softly together about phenomenology and heuristics.

Little did I realize what this brief *jeu d'esprit* would ultimately lead to. I was already halfway down the path toward what Sherlockians call "playing the game" and what outsiders dismiss as spoof scholarship. Still, it came as a surprise when I was suddenly invited to deliver the Distinguished Speaker's Lecture for the year 2000 at the annual "birthday weekend" of The Baker Street Irregulars.

"It Is the Unofficial Force"

⌧ The Baker Street Irregulars (BSI) was established in 1934 by literary journalist Christopher Morley as a sodality devoted to honoring the greatest of all consulting detectives, Sherlock Holmes of 221B Baker Street. The group takes its name from the ragamuffin street urchins who occasionally assist the detective; as Holmes says, they can "go everywhere, see everything, overhear everyone."

In particular, the Irregulars and various local "scion societies"—the Copper Beeches of Philadelphia, the Speckled Band of Boston, the Red Circle of Washington, the Illustrious Clients of Indianapolis—have for decades been bringing together enthusiasts to play a peculiar, if addictive game, founded on the premise that Sherlock Holmes really lived and Dr. John H. Watson recorded his investigations. (Arthur Conan Doyle merely served as Watson's literary agent, and contrived to take more credit than he deserved.) Alas, the good doctor was prone to romanticize his friend, misremember details, and make mistakes in chronology, thus leaving room for ongoing conjecture about Holmes's family background, early career, that three-year disappearance in the 1890s (the Great Hiatus), and the Master's eventual retirement to the Sussex Downs. There, you will recall, this precise thinking machine devoted himself to keeping bees and completing his masterwork, *The Whole Art of Detection*.

How, you may ask, does one make a game of all this? By filling in the gaps in Watson's narrative and by deliberate, clever misreading—the French deconstructionists have nothing on the Irregulars when it comes to finding latent, suppressed meanings hidden in "endless minutiae." For instance, could that mysterious government official Mycroft Holmes—Sherlock's older, extremely indolent, and smarter brother—be the original M of British Intelligence? Or might "this central exchange, this clearing house" be the guardian of a computer (or even himself an anthropomorphic computer) created by Charles Babbage? Of course, the pleasure in such speculation derives from the researcher's ability to build a convincing, seemingly airtight case: Manly Wade Wellman, for instance, determined with inflexible logic that Sherlock Holmes was the father of P. G. Wodehouse's all-knowing valet Jeeves.

Is all this clear so far? As H. W. Bell observed long ago, "the subject is vastly complicated and correspondingly amusing." Besides these narrative gaps into which a scholar can read deeply (or even plunge to his doom), the canon's fifty-six stories and four novels propound myriad other matters upon which to exercise one's ingenuity. What kind of snake was the Speckled Band? How many times did Dr. Watson marry? (Evidence suggests at least two wives; Trevor Hall uncovered five, not necessarily excessive for a man of hearty appetites whose admitted knowledge of women "extended over many nations and three separate continents.") Which university did Holmes attend, Oxford or Cambridge? (Christopher Morley proposed that Holmes undertook postgraduate studies at Johns Hopkins.) Just establishing the proper order for the various cases can be the work of a lifetime: There have been at least fifteen separate attempts among the Irregulars' micro-chronologists to clarify Watson's incoherencies.

These days, even though The Baker Street Irregulars accepts Doyleans—people who regard the Holmes exploits as stories written by the author of *The Lost World*—it still doesn't encourage this misguided approach. Yet at that time I was, if anything, a Doylean. Why, then, had the affable Michael F. Whelan, the current "Wiggins," as the head of the BSI is termed, asked me to address the society in the new millennium? It is true that during the 1990s I had become friends with Jon Lellenberg, a Pentagon defense specialist, who was also a representative for the Conan Doyle estate in North America and the author of five volumes in the archival history of The Baker Street Irregulars. Perhaps Lellenberg—who once noted that the BSI began as "a cocktail party at the Hotel Duane, on Madison Avenue, on January 6, 1934," and that that party, "in the large sense, is still going on today"—had detected my liking for Tanqueray martinis, literary talk, and good company. Making the obvious deduction, he had recommended me as a suitable speaker for the BSI.

That long New York weekend of January 13–15, 2000, certainly never stinted on the sluicing and carousing, as well as being hectic with numerous social and professional events. Highpoints included a breakfast meeting of the advisory board for the Sherlock Holmes Collection housed at the University of Minnesota; the William Gillette

Lunch, named after the actor who played Holmes on the stage for forty years; and not least, a superb performance by Roger Llewellyn in David Stuart Davies's almost too wrenching one-man play, *Sherlock Holmes—The Last Act.*

Everyone was unnervingly genial and welcoming. The BSI dealers' room offered Sherlockian pins, tote bags, ties, magnets, watches, calendars, CDs, playbills, cookie tins, statuettes, deerstalkers, and books (including *The Sign of the Four* written out in Pitman shorthand and a first edition of the *Memoirs* for $675). Saturday afternoon the Wodehousean subgroup, the Clients of Adrian Mulliner, even presented a dramatization of a "Schlock Homes" misadventure about the disappearance of the pig "Empress of Bloatings." Late that same night I sat up—until the canonical hour of 2:21 a.m.—listening to stories told by science fiction eminence Poul Anderson and chatting with members of ASH, the notorious Adventuresses of Sherlock Holmes.

Certainly, the actual BSI banquet, held at the Union League Club and restricted to the group's three hundred or so invested members and selected friends, was replete with wit, nostalgia, and affection. Beforehand, we toasted Eleanor O'Connor as "*The* Woman," that year's living avatar of Irene Adler ("To Sherlock Holmes she is always *the* Woman"), making O'Connor the latest in a BSI tradition that started with ecdysiast Gypsy Rose Lee. A gigantic and ancient scanning camera then took a panoramic picture of the assembled host, garbed in black tie and evening dress. We recited the responses to the Musgrave Ritual: "Whose was it? His who is gone. Who shall have it? He who will come. . . ." We even belted out the naughty BSI anthem, "We Never Mention Aunt Clara":

She used to sing hymns in the old village choir.
She used to teach Sunday School class.
Of playing the organ she never would tire,
Those dear days are over, alas!
At church on the organ she'd practice and play,
The Preacher would pump up and down,
His wife caught them back of the organ one day,
And that's why Aunt Clara left town.
    We never mention Aunt Clara;
    Her picture is turned to the wall.
    Though she lives on the French Riviera
    Mother says she is dead to us all . . .

Later, we chatted and joked through a meal replicating the first 1934 dinner, all the courses alluding to canonical stories, starting with Oysters "Dying Detective" and ending with Cafe "Black Peter." The noble program booklet itself was illustrated by Scott Bond, known for his Sherlockian cartoons in the *Baker Street Journal*, and the commemorative swag bag for each member included the special Sherlockian issue of *Ellery Queen's Mystery Magazine*, the Christmas annual of the Norwegian Explorers, and a clutch of keepsake monographs. During the more serious part of the evening, we listened to a panel of doctors discuss the efficacy of the canon's various poisons, the sexual elements in "The Creeping Man" (the phrase "Come at once" has lost its boyish innocence), and the possibility that Professor Moriarty might have suffered from Parkinson's disease. Two iconoclasts then actually proposed a millennial revision of the BSI's Constitutional Buy-Laws, so spelled (and based on the need to keep the drink flowing). They were hooted down. The Buy-Laws famously conclude: "All other business shall be left for the monthly meeting." Pause. "There shall be no monthly meeting."

At the end of "His Last Bow" a grave Holmes turns to his faithful Watson—"the one fixed point in a changing age"—and unexpectedly says, "Stand with me here upon the terrace, for it may be the last quiet talk that we shall ever have." To stand upon the terrace has, over the years, grown synonymous with the somber portion of the BSI dinner, the honoring of those members who have "passed beyond the Reichenbach." Following these memorial tributes, the leisurely evening—it was nearly midnight—wound up with the "birthday honors list" at which Whelan announced the BSI's new members, each being granted an investiture name drawn from the Sacred Writings. These names are typically chosen to harmonize with the honoree's profession or personality. For instance, that night the actor Douglas Wilmer was invested as "The Lyceum Theater" and Dr. Fred Kittle, a leading Doylean and owner of the original manuscript of *The White Company,* was granted the investiture name of Jack Stapleton, the naturalist and collector of *The Hound of the Baskervilles.* Kittle has since donated his vast Conan Doyle holdings to Chicago's Newberry Library.

My actual talk, which took place the Thursday evening before the Friday banquet, started innocently enough. An initial discussion of Watson's narrative style and the canon's "atmospheric emanations" segued into a reminiscence of my boyhood reading of the Sherlock Holmes stories. This led in turn to some reflections on the pervasive literary influence of such Irregulars as Victor Starrett, Christopher Morley, Frederic Dannay, and Rex Stout, not overlooking such lesser lights as Franklin D. Roosevelt and Harry Truman (both of whom were invested BSI members). And then I sprang my surprise.

It has long been remarked that many of Holmes's enemies possess names starting with M—for example, Professor Moriarty, Colonel Sebastian Moran, the master blackmailer Charles Augustus Milverton. Critics have also noticed the canon's various trios: the Three Students, the Three Garridebs, the three Mrs. Watsons, the three Moriarty brothers. Oddly suggestive, isn't it? For there is one other notable Sherlockian trio, associated with a name in M: Christopher, Frank, and Felix Morley, of course, the founders of The Baker Street Irregulars.

Suppose, I reasoned, Professor Moriarty, like Holmes, had survived the tumble into the Reichenbach Falls. What better place to rebuild his criminal empire than America, far from the prying eyes of Sherlock Holmes and Scotland Yard? Being good students of Machiavelli, Moriarty and his brothers would instantly grasp that the best possible cover for a newly revivified crime syndicate would be an organization ostensibly devoted to . . . honoring their greatest enemy.

Naturally, I didn't reveal all my evidence for the "Secret History" of The Baker Street Irregulars. And naturally, some of my listeners may have regarded this kind of theorizing as sheer madness. But was it? Then how do you explain the death threat I received the next morning? It was printed in block letters on stationery from the Algonquin Hotel: "Mr. Dirda: You are more clever than I thought. You have uncovered the secret mission of the BSI. You will have to be eliminated."

The note was signed with a single initial—M, of course. It was obviously from that blackguard Moriarty or possibly Colonel Moran, the "second most dangerous man in London" and, you will recall, the best heavy-game shot that the Eastern British Empire ever produced. So either the Napoleon of Crime himself was after me, or his chief enforcer, a cold-blooded assassin who currently favored the almost noiseless air-gun, an elegant weapon designed by the blind German mechanic, Von Herder. Clearly I would have to stay away from lighted windows and hope that my slight knowledge of baritsu, the Japanese system of wrestling, would be as useful to me as it had been to Sherlock Holmes at the Reichenbach Falls.

Do I need to say that I had an absolutely wonderful time at my first BSI weekend? To mingle quotes from *The Sign of the Four* and *The Valley of Fear*, it was "rather an irregular proceeding" but very much an evening "for fraternal refreshment and for harmony." Most of all, I felt connected to an otherwise vanished era of literary bonhomie and frivolity. Invited back the following January—the BSI always holds its annual dinner around January 6, the birthday of the Master—I had to decline due to a previous commitment. However, that spring I was able to attend a formal banquet held to honor the 100th anniversary of the first appearance, in the *Strand Magazine*, of *The Hound of the Baskervilles*.

The great feast took place on May 12 at the CIA—in this case, the familiar initials stood for the Culinary Institute of America, located in Hyde Park, New York. The evening's festivities were genially presided over by the CIA's director, the master chef and BSI member Frederic H. Sonnenschmidt (coauthor, with his fellow Irregular, Julia Carlson Rosenblatt, of *Dining with Sherlock Holmes*). Fritz recreated a seventeenth-century saturnalia complete with roast boar hoisted in on a pole by sturdy young CIA students. The wicked Sir Hugo Baskerville would have been right at home. There were, naturally, a series of toasts, and I was asked to present one to the Hound itself. I went all out:

Ladies and gentlemen, please raise your glasses.

As haunting as Anubis, the dog-faced Egyptian god of the dead.

As fearsome as Cerberus, who guards the Gates of Hell.

As chilling as the ghostly banshee pack of the Devil's Wild Hunt.

More relentless than any backwood's Southern sheriff's bloodhound.

More powerful than the gigantic mastiffs and Rottweilers of urban legend.

More savage than a Pit Bull trained to kill without mercy.

Not man's best friend, but his most vivid nightmare.

Not his faithful companion but a demon of slavering ferocity, an engine of human destruction, a monster from the id.

Such is this spectral fiend in canine form, this Thing that came out of the swamp at night to spread horror and violent murder over the moors.

Its story appeared for the first time one hundred years ago this August. Its legend has grown over the past century so that the mere iteration of its name still makes even the most jaded reader's hair stand on end.

Just recall, for a moment, your own first encounter with this archetypal creature of the night, this instrument of diabolical revenge, as inescapable and relentless as the dreaded Furies themselves.

Ladies and gentlemen, friends of the immortal Sherlock Holmes and Dr. Watson, let us offer a toast to that most hideously terrifying yet ultimately pitiable beast of the brooding rocks and mires of spooky Dartmoor. Let us drink this night of all nights to The Hound of the Baskervilles.

In 2002 I was again invited to the birthday weekend, and that year was thrilled to hear Mike Whelan intone the ringing phrases composed by his predecessor Edgar W. Smith—"In witness whereof, and in recognition of distinguished service rendered in the Cause of keeping green the Master's memory, there is affixed hereto the Canonical recompense of the Irregular Shilling"—as he granted me the investiture name of Langdale Pike. Pike appears in "The Three Gables" as a gossip columnist who sits in the bow window of his club and waits for all the news and secrets of London to come to him. And they do. As Holmes says in that story, "Now, Watson, this is a case for Langdale Pike, and I am going to see him now."

As a supposedly well-connected literary journalist, I soon inherited the responsibility of recruiting further distinguished speakers, and in the subsequent five years roped in John Berendt, author not only of *Midnight in the Garden of Good and Evil* but also of an introduction to the *Adventures of Sherlock Holmes*; artist Gahan Wilson, noted for his many Holmesian (and Lovecraftian) cartoons for *Playboy*; crime novelist Laurie R. King, whose young heroine Mary Russell becomes, as the title of the first book in an ongoing series has it, *The Beekeeper's Apprentice,* and later Sherlock Holmes's wife; LeRoy Lad Panek, one of the most esteemed historians and critics of the detective story; and Sir Christopher Frayling, then head of Britain's Arts Council but a longtime devotee of Holmes and of *The Hound of the Baskervilles* in particular.

While the BSI dinner itself is largely restricted to invested members, the noisy multitude does include a couple of dozen hopeful aspirants and special guests. Early on I invited my friends Neil Gaiman—chronicler of "The Sandman" and author of the Sherlockian-Lovecraftian pastiche "A Study in Emerald"—and the novelist Peter Straub, as well as two women of letters, also close friends: Alice Turner, longtime fiction editor of *Playboy*, and Michele Slung, author of *Crime on Her Mind* and many other books. Need I add that another good time was had by all? I had begun to see why the BSI had been going strong for so many years and why it flourishes still today.

"I Play the Game for the Game's Own Sake"

After being invested in the Irregulars I soon took to answering my phone at *Book World* with a jaunty "Dirda—the second most dangerous man in Washington." That gave people pause (and some tried to guess who was the most dangerous). Better still, I was also now eligible to participate in that most exclusive of all local dining sodalities: the Half Pay Club, open only to DC area members of the BSI.

Like science fiction and fantasy fans, Sherlockians enjoy carousing as often as possible. From the

Scowrers and Molly Maguires of San Francisco to the Six Napoleons of Baltimore, almost every major city possesses a scion society, and nearly all these welcome anyone interested in Sherlock Holmes and Dr. Watson. It goes without saying that their curious names derive from the Sacred Writings. In Canada, for example, the Bootmakers of Toronto are so called because Sir Henry Baskerville's boots—a key element in *The Hound of the Baskervilles*—were made by "Meyers, Toronto."

At all these bodies, people play "the game," or more formally "the grand game"—that is, they speculate upon the historical gaps in the canon or attempt to harmonize its chronological confusions. The great bible of the game was for many years W. S. Baring-Gould's *Annotated Sherlock Holmes*. This classic has now been updated, enlarged, and modified by Leslie S. Klinger in his Wessex Press *Sherlock Holmes Reference Library*—minutely annotated editions of the nine canonical books—and his more popular, and abundantly illustrated, *New Annotated Sherlock Holmes*, published by Norton in three substantial hardcover volumes.

Yet even these mammoth tomes contain only a fraction of the voluminous Sherlockian scholarship indexed by Ronald De Waal in his vast bibliography, *The Universal Sherlock Holmes*. Despite some rival claimants for the honor, the generally accepted starting point for the game is the 1911 paper "Studies in the Literature of Sherlock Holmes," delivered by Ronald Knox while a student at Oxford. Here, the youthful Knox—in later life a distinguished Catholic savant—compared the Sacred Writings to Platonic dialogues and Greek tragedies, proposed a deutero-Watson, addressed the possibility of spurious adventures, expatiated at length upon the symbolic importance of Watson's bowler hat and, most important of all, provided an eleven-point morphology of the Sherlockian tale, organized according to Greek rhetorical categories. Any authentic Sherlockian story, writes Knox, begins with "the Prooimion, a homely Baker Street scene, with invaluable personal touches, and sometimes a demonstration by the detective," then nearly always advances to the "Ichneusis, or personal investigation, often including the famous floor-walk on hands and knees," and ends with the Metamenusis "in which Holmes describes what his clues were and how he followed them." The whole narrative is then capped by an "Epilogos," which usually takes the form of a "quotation from some standard author."

Perhaps awed by Knox's formidable example, Sherlockian studies lay relatively quiescent for the following two decades. But by the early 1930s a Golden Age had dawned with a series of ground-breaking works of Baker Street scholarship and "dialectical hullaballoo." Landmark volumes of this era include Cambridge don S. C. Roberts's *Dr. Watson: Prolegomena to the Study of a Biographical Problem* (1931), and *The Private Life of Sherlock Holmes* by Vincent Starrett (1934), probably the single most important study of the great detective and the canon. Over the years other cornerstone works would appear: Edgar W. Smith's *Profile by Gaslight*, Dorothy L. Sayers's *Unpopular Opinions*, James E. Holroyd's *Baker Street Byways* and *Seventeen Steps to Baker Street*, T. S. Blakeney's *Sherlock Holmes: Fact or Fiction,* H. W. Bell's *Baker Street Studies*, the Starrett-edited *221B Baker Street*, and Christopher Morley's *Holmes and Watson: A Textbook of Friendship.*

Today, most contemporary scholarship appears in bulletins of the larger scions, the publications of the Sherlock Holmes Society of London, or the *Baker Street Journal*, the official quarterly of the BSI. Of the *BSJ* it has been affectionately observed, "Never has so much been written by so many for so few." Nonetheless, if you possess the right turn of mind, these instances of patient textual scholarship in the service of often mind-boggling flights of fancy can be challenging fun. These are, after all, *jeux d'esprit* in the best sense. You need to be as clever as possible, while supporting even the most outrageous hypotheses with cogent reasoning and seemingly irrefutable evidence. Dorothy Sayers always insisted that one should play the game without even the hint of a smile.

Sometimes that's not a problem, as when attentive reading determines that Holmes possessed considerable fluency in American English, French, German, Italian, Norwegian, and Gaelic, at least a smattering of Russian, Swedish, Dutch, and Chinese, and some knowledge of ancient Cornish and Chaldean. Now you may well ask: What is the evidence for Holmes's acquaintance with Cornish and Chaldean? In this case, the answer is quite simple. In "The Devil's Foot," the care-worn detective attempts a recuperative holiday, during which, Watson recalls, "the ancient Cornish language . . . arrested his attention and he had, I remember, conceived the idea that it was akin to the Chaldean."

Lest you imagine that all this learned speculation smacks of hagiography, that is certainly not the case. For instance, D. Martin Dakin—one of the most astute commentators on the canon—forcefully criticizes Holmes's behavior in a brief essay titled "Holmes's Bad Deed." "Need I say," writes Dakin in these pages of *A Sherlock Holmes Commentary*, "that I refer to the shocking affair . . . where Holmes committed the unpardonable offence of trifling with a woman's affections?" In "Charles Augustus Milverton" the detective disguises himself as a plumber named Escott and woos a young servant to the point of becoming engaged to her. Dakin points out that the chivalrous Watson was stung to remonstrance: "But the girl, Holmes?" . . . "You can't help it, my dear Watson. You must play your cards as best you can when such a stake is on the table." Dakin continues:

> This plea of the end justifying the means has been the excuse for half the shoddy deeds in history. And what was the stake on the table? The successful marriage of Lady Eva Brackwell! We may well ask if the happiness of a housemaid was not just as important as that of a society lady—even if she was the most beautiful debutante of the season. No doubt Victorian society did not think so; but one might have hoped that Holmes, especially after his cavalier attitude to certain other VIPs, might have been above such snobbery.

It's hard to disagree with Dakin in judging Holmes's behavior in this instance as ethically deplorable. That said, most Sherlockian theorizing does tend to be delightfully tongue-in-cheek, playfully imaginative rather than censorious. Consider just a few explanations of the true meaning of the events at the Reichenbach Falls. Ronald Knox sought to prove that Mycroft was actually in league with Moriarty and that our Sherlock never returned from the Great Hiatus. Instead, he was replaced by a second-rate lookalike, perhaps a cousin named Sherrinford. Jason Rouby conjectured that Holmes let Moriarty go at the Reichenbach and that the reformed master criminal went on to pursue a career in law enforcement in the United States, taking the name J. Edgar Hoover. C. Arnold Johnson, by contrast, hypothesized that Moriarty returned to London as Fu Manchu, while William Leonard determined that Moriarty survived because he was actually the undead Count Dracula.

Various commentators have linked Sherlock Holmes romantically with Irene Adler (W. S. Baring-Gould's *Sherlock Holmes of Baker Street*, a *vie romancée*, ends with the dying detective murmuring her name), but other women have been suggested as possible paramours: Lizzie

Borden, Countess Dracula, and even an abominable snowwoman (during the travels in Tibet). Someone writing as Vivian Darkbloom—an anagram for Vladimir Nabokov—has suggested that in "The Speckled Band" Holmes deliberately murders the evil-seeming Dr. Grimesby Roylott "to clear the way for an illicit liaison" with Roylott's supposed victim, young Helen Stoner. John Hogan even builds a case that Sherlock's brother Mycroft helped found the Playboy Club of London.

Obviously much of this is just a peculiar kind of fun, like Robert J. Schutz's habit, according to his obituary in the *Baker Street Journal*, of "creating catalog cards for Holmes's writings and surreptitiously inserting them in catalog drawers of libraries he visited." Similarly, the "Wants and Offers" section at the back of early issues of the *BSJ* are packed with in-jokes. Those from a single issue of 1946 include the following:

> I want to meet the worst man in New York. Object: hands across the sea. CAM, Appledore Towers, Hampstead.

> I offer excellent blend Egyptian cigarettes, boxes of 100 special price 3 guineas. Ionides, Alexandria.

I want: Information concerning the whereabouts of James Phillimore. Bureau of Missing Persons.

All these may sound deeply enigmatic, unless you recognize the allusions. The initials CAM obviously belong to Charles Augustus Milverton, "the worst man in London," Ionides' cigarettes play an important role in "The Golden Pince-Nez," and high among the most tantalizing of Holmes's unpublished cases is that of James Phillimore "who, stepping back into his house to get an umbrella, was never more seen in this world."

Today BSI members and friends help organize regular conferences at the Sherlock Holmes Library of the University of Minnesota, Indiana University (the location of the Lilly Library with many Irregular associations), the Toronto Public Library (home to North America's greatest Arthur Conan Doyle collection), and Harvard's Houghton Library, which houses the archives of the BSI itself. Like many long-established organizations, The Baker Street Irregulars, though flourishing, does worry about the graying of its membership; hence the Beacon Society (for junior Sherlockians), school writing contests, and similar initiatives to encourage young people to read and discuss the stories. Nonetheless, a coterie of distinguished Irregulars believes that the BSI of the twenty-first century has already grown too large and consequently lost the intimate camaraderie characteristic of meetings in the 1930s and '40s. Several of these Sherlockians and Doyleans now hold their own dinners and cocktail parties during the birthday weekend, keeping the numbers small, the company lively, and the drink flowing.

"A Case for Langdale Pike"

After having presented several brief and light-hearted talks at various BSI functions, I finally felt ready to enter the lists of Sherlockian speculation and scholarship. Because of my investiture name, it was probably inevitable that I should explore the background and complex hidden life of gossip columnist Langdale Pike. My paper, originally presented at a University of Minnesota conference ("Victorian Secrets and Edwardian Enigmas"), shocked even some of the most weather-beaten Irregulars, though appalled may be the word I really want. I opened, slowly. with an account of my serendipitous discovery of an exceedingly rare volume entitled *A Case for Langdale Pike*. Only gradually did I unveil the full import of this book on our understanding of Sherlock Holmes. What follows are just a few highlights. A more complete text of the paper, including photographs, footnotes, and an exchange of letters about the reference to "the late Sir Harry Flashman," may be found in *Canadian Holmes: The Journal of the Bootmakers of Toronto*, Fall and Winter 2007.

"A Case for Langdale Pike"

To many students of the canon "The Three Gables" is arguably the most controversial of Dr. Watson's reminiscences of the great detective. In fact, Holmes appears so out of character that some Sherlockians, such as Martin Dakin, have regarded the entire account as spurious. Les Klinger gives a full survey of the story's oddities in the commentary included in his magisterial *New Annotated Sherlock Holmes*.

In brief, though, "The Three Gables" describes an uncomfortable case involving London toughs, a dead diplomat, a robbery, and a Spanish adventuress, the celebrated beauty Isadora Klein. But what interests us here is the following: At a point of crisis and uncertainty Holmes suddenly, unexpectedly turns to his faithful companion and says, "Now, Watson, this is a case for Langdale Pike, and I am going to see him now. When I get back I may be clearer in the matter.'

Watson proceeds to explain:

> I saw no more of Holmes during the day, but I could well imagine how he spent it, for Langdale Pike was his human book of reference upon all matters of social scandal. This strange, languid creature spent his waking hours in the bow window of a St James's Street club, and was the receiving-station, as well as the transmitter, for all the gossip of the Metropolis. He made, it was said, a four-figure income by the paragraphs which he contributed every week to the garbage papers which cater for an inquisitive public. If ever, far down in the turbid depths of London life, there was some strange swirl or eddy, it was marked with automatic exactness by this human dial upon the surface. Holmes discreetly helped Langdale to knowledge, and on occasion was helped in turn.

This is, obviously, an eye-opening passage on several counts.

First, excluding the nonpareil Sherlock, the languid Pike is clearly the third member in what might be called the canon's triumvirate of masterminds, the others being Professor Moriarty, with his finger on the criminal pulse of Britain, and Mycroft Holmes, that human computer who gathers and analyzes British intelligence from around the world. What Moriarty is to crime and Mycroft to every sort of foreign and domestic intrigue, Pike is, apparently, to society.

Second, Langdale Pike has made himself wealthy through his vast knowledge and acquaintance, though there is a tinge of disapproval in Watson's voice when he describes how the man supplies insider information and scandal to the newspapers. The comments about the "turbid depths" also imply that Pike's knowledge isn't always just gossip, but something far more unsavory, the kind of information that might turn up in a modern investigative reporter's notes or in a private eye's report—sexual indiscretions, financial shenanigans, every manner of secret vice.

And finally, Watson himself knows Pike personally, for he refers to him familiarly as Langdale.

This is all we ever learn about Langdale Pike from John Watson, or indeed from any other source but one. Happily, there exists a full column and a half devoted to the journalist's life in the multivolume *Dictionary of National Biography*. Or rather it did exist: for some unaccountable reason, Pike has been left out of the most recent revision, available only in digital form through subscription. But if you can turn up an old copy of the thick DNB volume covering deaths between 1914 and 1925—no easy task, by the way—you should find the following entry:

Pike, **Langdale** (1844–1923), London journalist and man about town. Born in the United States at Oberlin, Ohio, on January 16, 1844. Son of Lyman Townsend Pike, professor of Old Testament theology at Oberlin Seminary, by his wife Ann Elizabeth Hall, abolitionist organizer and author of *The Call to Action*. Siblings include elder brother Gen. Biltmore Pike, commander of the Western Reserve volunteers (killed in action, Battle of the Wilderness, awarded posthumous Medal of Honor) and younger sister Miss Saralinda Hartley Pike (coloratura soprano, best known for originating the role of Quilla in Pozzo's *I Vitelloni*).

Upon completing his undergraduate degree in classics (Harvard, with distinction, 1861), Pike accepted a roving commission from the U.S. Army during the War Between the States. Little more is known about his activities before 1880, when he arrived in England as the secretary and manager of Miss Lillie Langtry. Thereafter he worked, in various capacities, in theatrical and artistic circles, where his associates included Henry Irving, Bram Stoker,

Miss Irene Adler, Oscar Wilde, Enoch Soames, Frank Harris, Miss Catherine Walters, and Henry James.

During the mid-1890s Pike was employed as an assistant to celebrated journalist W. T. Stead. Later, like his friends Israel Zangwill and Arthur Morrison, Pike helped expose the desperate conditions of London's slums and the turbid depths of the city's underworld. He was briefly engaged to Jennie Jerome (later Mrs. Randolph Churchill).

Using the unlikely pen name Henry E. Dudeney, Pike for many years contributed a monthly puzzle feature, called "Perplexities," to the *Strand Magazine*. The column was widely admired, particularly by the eminent mathematician James Moriarty, who frequently recommended it to his students and associates as "extremely instructive"; he once called its author the greatest puzzlist of all time. As two regular and prominent *Strand* contributors, Pike and Dr. John H. Watson eventually met at a soirée given by the magazine's founder George Newnes. Watson, whom Pike later employed as his physician, introduced the American journalist to the well-known consulting detective Mr. Sherlock Holmes. In an amusing passage of his reminiscences, Sir Arthur Sullivan speaks with considerable goodhearted raillery about a duet, performed during a charity concert at the embassy of Bohemia, in which Pike on the piano accompanied Holmes on the violin.

In later years Langdale Pike became an increasingly well-known gentleman about town, dining out frequently among the highest echelons of London society, spending long afternoons over piquet with his friend A. J. Raffles at one or another of their clubs (White's, the Athenaeum, the Savage, the Diogenes), and regularly attending concerts at Covent Garden. With the outbreak of World War I, the American-born Pike joined Henry James in taking up British citizenship. (It has often been rumored that James's *nouvelle* "The Social Whirl" is largely based on a somewhat *louche* anecdote about Pike, related to the novelist by Isadora Klein, now Lady Lomond.)

Before his sudden and unexpected death— from unknown causes, while on an archaeological holiday in Denmark with Dr. M. R. James, Provost of Eton—Pike took great pains to destroy all his papers. His only publication extant is an exceedingly rare volume, the privately printed *A Case for Langdale Pike* (not present in the British Museum Library). Following his express instructions, Pike's body was cremated, his ashes scattered, and no monument or memorial allowed to show that he had ever lived.

Now, this brief summary is just about all that can be readily discovered concerning Langdale Pike's life and career. It has been rumored that Pike's brother Biltmore, the army general, is mentioned prominently in *The Flashman Papers*, but unfortunately the volumes relating the Civil War triumphs of England's greatest soldier have yet to be released by their editor.

Yet even if this is all we know about Pike the man, we do know a bit more about his book. Before its last-minute deletion from *Queen's Quorum*, an annotated list of the 100 greatest works of detection, the writing team of Frederick Dannay and Manfred Lee (aka Ellery Queen) carefully described *A Case for Langdale Pike*:

> *A Case for Langdale Pike*. By Langdale Pike. Published in 1907, by Savoy Press, in an edition of 10 large-paper copies (on hand-made Barcham-Green paper) and 100 ordinary copies, all signed by the author. 164 pages. Exotic cover design by Sidney Sime. Frontispiece photograph of author by Alvin Langdon Coburn.
>
> Neither as decadent as the Prince Zaleski stories of M. P. Shiel (q.v.) nor as sensationalistic as the Sherlock Holmes tales (q.v.), the eight short narratives in *A Case for Langdale Pike* display mastery of every variety of detective story, including the

impossible murder, the gothic thriller, the witty comedy of manners, and that form so beloved by Agatha Christie (q.v.), the revelation of the least likely character as the villain. Several of the stories possess a surprisingly gamey character for the time—there is more than one example of "a woman who did"—while others may well be fictionalizations of actual historical incidents. One or two are constructed like coolly logical puzzles (it is perhaps worth noting, in this regard, that under a pseudonym Pike authored a popular mathematical recreations column for the *Strand Magazine*). All are composed in a digressive, somewhat long-winded style, occasionally reminiscent of late Henry James or early stream of consciousness. The eponymous title story, which opens the collection, is also notable for its high degree of personal history.

This volume is of the greatest rarity, since Langdale Pike seems to have changed his mind about the book, eventually paying to have the stock destroyed. Only a few copies—perhaps just two or three—are known to have survived this strange holocaust. Legal embargo even now prevents the volume from being reprinted. Still, the compilers of *Queen's Quorum* have read *A Case for Langdale Pike* and one of them judges it a tour de force of imaginative ratiocination.

Before I present the opening pages of Pike's text, I want to direct your attention to its curious, yet suggestive, acknowledgments:

> I would like to thank for their particular contributions to the following pages: His Royal Highness Prince Florizel of Bohemia; Clarence, Lord Emsworth; the late Sir Harry Flashman; Professor G. E. Challenger; the Doctors Nikola and Thorndyke; Mr Oswald Bastable; Mrs Godfrey Norton; and, of course, my dear friends in the legal offices of Escott, Altamont and Sigerson.

The book also carries this dedication: "To Frederick, Lord Ickenham; Mr. A. V. Laider; and Mr. Joseph Jorkens, this form of flattery, in homage to their immortal example: The truth is in the telling." The title page then includes a brief epigraph, taken from Enoch Soames's last collection, *Fungoids*: "Thou art, who has not been!"

Lest we delay any further, here are the opening pages from a volume that will change forever how we think about Sherlock Holmes:

> Langdale Pike stretched out on a divan, while outside his club's bow window the city of London stretched out before him. Lunch with Saintsbury always meant good book talk—and good wine.

But clearly he had, as usual, drunk too much of the Poincaré '93—or was it the Chateau Guizot '86? No matter. He felt sleepy.

Pike closed his eyes and began to daydream. He had certainly come a long way since those days back in Oberlin. Who would have thought it? His poor father had wanted him to go into the church like the old professor's classmates Charles Finney and Henry Ward Beecher; his mother, despite her fiery speeches about the rights of women, had hoped he would marry that quiet little mouse in Massachusetts . . . what was her name . . . she wrote odd little poems . . . Emily something. He couldn't remember.

Then the war had come. It was there he'd first met Flashy, whom his brother couldn't stand. Said the man was little more than a scoundrel and a poltroon, but then Biltmore never was a good judge of character. Poor Bilty. He disapproved of his little brother becoming a spy, too: "Damn it, Lang, it's no better than being a common sneak." Still, Bilty was always glad for the information he managed to acquire.

So many, many memories. Big Brother would have been even more appalled by his later life as the paid "companion" of that singing whore, as he would have doubtless called Lillie. Sis had just started her own far more respectable operatic career—hadn't yet met that Pozzo—and she introduced him to the Jersey Lily. From the moment their eyes met over dinner, an understanding passed between them, and that very evening he'd accompanied her back to her hotel room. . . . What was it he'd later read in Flaubert about the Queen of Sheba: "I am not a woman. I am a world." That was Lillie.

Pike dozed. Her European tour had brought him to London, and he took to the city immediately. The theatre, the music halls, the dinner parties. Before long, he was earning the occasional guinea by writing for *Tit-Bits*. Journalism, as people were starting to call it, suited his background and odd skills. What's more, in the years before Holmes grew so famous, people had often come to him with their little problems. There was the sudden disappearance of poor Soames, which little Max claimed was "the work of the devil." Poppycock. He'd realized right off that the poet had fled to France to escape his creditors. Best thing he could have done. And what about Conan Doyle's hysterical wife, who was convinced that her husband was in love with a younger woman? More nonsense. Conan Doyle was as true an English gentleman as Harry Flashman:

blade true, steel sharp, or whatever the old saying was. Just as soon imagine him believing in fairies as being unfaithful.

Fairies. That reminded him of that sordid kidnapping case, those three children. What was their name? Oh yes, Darling. He'd delivered the ransom and kept quiet when the kids, dressed in nothing but their nightgowns, maintained that a magic little boy had taught them to fly and taken them to a land far away full of pirates and Indians and crocodiles and special cakes. People naturally dismissed the whole business as overactive imaginations. Fact is, thought Pike, he was pretty sure they were all high on opium or cocaine and that sister Wendy was playing with some Peter in more ways than one. But no point in ruining a young girl's reputation.

Maybe he really was an old cynic. Everyone told him so. Hell, he was nothing but a hard-headed practical Yankee. That's probably why the insurance companies turned to him so often. Over at St Wulfram's Church in Abbeville, they blathered about the death of that antiquarian scholar Karswell, crushed by some falling masonry as "an act of God" when it was clearly worker negligence. They shouldn't have allowed tourists so near the renovation site. When he investigated that so-called ghost ship at Whitby, it was obvious too that the dead captain had gone mad. You could see the horror in his face. Pity that big dog had escaped and not been found. Probably had rabies and been the cause of the entire shipboard tragedy.

So many cases. That border rivalry between Graustark and Ruritania—nearly came to open conflict. Those perverted accusations against the Duke of Clarence when the man couldn't even handle a pocket-knife! And, worst of all, the never-ending persecution of poor Moriarty. The desperate man actually pleaded on bended knees for help. Here was a mathematical genius who had presented a brilliant paper on the dynamics of the asteroid to a standing ovation from the Royal Society, and this was the thanks he got. That whole Cambridge crowd—Rutherford, Bertie Russell, little G. H. Hardy—looked quite put out by it. Then, shortly afterward, this hate campaign. Even Sherlock had got caught up in that madness. Academic jealousy, nothing more than that. He'd seen it all before back at Harvard.

And Moriarty was a real scholar, too, not like that Van Dusen fellow, always popping round with his little thought experiments, trying to sound all jaunty and casual. "I say, Pike. I've got a teaser for you. Let's say you're a criminal, who is suddenly arrested and bunged away into one of those maximum security cells. Think the great puzzlist could figure a way to escape? Hmm. You could. Mind if I took a few notes?" Should never have told that charlatan professor about his authorship of the "Perplexities" column in the *Strand*. That was a mistake.

Like that night with Jennie. She'd made her choice and chosen Randolph. Bloody hell. But then a few years later, after that soppy poetry reading by that Irishman, more stuff about fairies and wild swans and golden apples of the sun, there had been a glass of champagne at Emerald Cunard's, then another and, well, one is only human. Funny to think that young Winston isn't just half American, but entirely American. Just so long as Randolph never knows.

Pike was starting to breathe regularly, falling into an afternoon slumber, when he heard a hesitant voice in his ear. It was that officious young waiter, the one who had actually confided that he was trying to better himself by reading Spinoza and memorizing Shakespeare! Apparently he aspired to become a gentleman's gentleman.

"Sir, Mr Pike, sir. I regret to intrude, but Mr Sherlock Holmes is here to see you. He seems quite insistent and, if I may say so, sir, somewhat agitated. Shall I send him away?"

"No, no. Send him in, uh—" What the deuce was his name; started with J? But the servant had already bowed and left the room.

Pike roused himself from his nostalgia. Bad sign, he thought, all this thinking about the past. That stick Strether—or was it Little Bilham?—had once told him, "I envy you, Lang. You've done so much with your life. I, by contrast, can only keep urging myself on—'Live life. Live all you can' and all that, I know it's a mistake not to. And yet I just can't quite seem to be anything but a proper Bostonian." Poor chap. He'd been visiting here from America, and had, in the most delicate way possible, wanted some information about a woman—an Isadora Klein sort—who had ensnared a rich young American. A common story. But always glad to help out a fellow Yank . . .

"Langdale."

Holmes looked the same as he nearly always did: slightly dazed and confused. Pike could never understand where the man's great reputation had come from. He'd heard rumors that Watson helped a lot more in those investigations than he was given credit for.

"Sherlock. Good to see you, old man. But you look, if I may say so, a bit downcast. Something to drink? No? Well, then, care to tell me about it?"

As Holmes breathlessly described what he called a truly confounding mystery involving the Spencer John gang and a house buyer who wanted everything left in the house untouched and the death of a young attaché in Italy, Pike listened with seeming inattention.

"So, old chap," finished up the frazzled detective, "I'm completely at a loss. Try as I might, I simply cannot figure out what's going on. If you can't help me, I really don't know whom else to turn to. I mean it—I'm at my wit's end. To tell you the truth, Langdale—and this mustn't get into the papers—the old reputation isn't what it used to be. My recent cases don't seem to be quite of the first caliber any more, and I'm afraid if I don't solve this one, I may really have to retire to the Sussex Downs and start keeping bees. And I hate bees. Did I tell you that while hiding out in Dartmoor once, I was stung five times? And they were huge creatures, bigger than wasps. Watson says I exaggerate, but he didn't see them. Personally I think the creatures must breed in the Grimpen Mire. That place isn't only a death-trap, it's a spawning ground. I should write a sharp letter to the local council, that's what I should do . . ."

"Sherlock, Sherlock," answered Pike. "Calm yourself. You always get so worked up over these trifles. It'll all turn out fine in the end. Trust me. Just relax a little. You really ought to take up some hobby besides the violin. That sawing away just encourages your morbid tendencies. Have you been practicing with your revolver in the way I showed you? I still remember that silly drunken evening when you asked me to demonstrate some western-style gunplay and I fanned a couple of initials into your study wall. Rather show-offy, I admit, but you could do that too, with practice."

"But, Langdale, what can I do right now about this latest enigma wrapped inside a conundrum? These mysteries seem to be getting harder and harder for me. Frankly, do you think I've lost my edge? Sometimes I wonder if my mind is giving way. I feel so inferior to these younger chaps like Hewitt and Thorndyke."

"Sherlock, *mon vieux*. You're a living legend. They'll never be a patch on the World's First and Greatest Consulting Detective. But right now here's what we'll do. This afternoon I'll get hold of young Wimsey: he's the head of what I call my

Belgrave Square Irregulars. I should have some answers for you by tea time. Will that be good enough? Please, no thanks are needed. It's the least I can do. But, tell me, how is John these days? I hear he's got a new wife. What is it— number two or number three?

Let me stop there, in the hope that I've whetted your interest in this unjustly neglected figure from the canon. There is, however, a postscript. Shortly after the publication of "A Case for Langdale Pike" in *Canadian Holmes*, I learned that the court-ordered inquest into Pike's death had surfaced in the Danish state archives. Unfortunately, the medical examiner's report had not yet been fully scanned (let alone translated), and all that is currently available online is a very brief précis. But this in itself is intensely suggestive.

Dr. M. R. James testified that he and Pike were investigating some ancient potsherds, upon which were scrawled unusually disturbing images. These apparently represented totemic gods or Great Old Ones, as they are commonly referred to by some of this northern region's rather inbred inhabitants. Pike, said James, had been retained by Miskatonic University in America to acquire further material relating to contemporary belief in these so-called gods and to any actual cult practices that might have survived into our own time.

I have, of course, written to the Danish state archivist requesting a photocopy of all the papers pertaining to the inquest and asking permission to publish an English translation.

▣ Permit me now to step away from playing the game to offer a possibly helpful note to readers. Loosely modeled after the pieces in Max Beerbohm's *Seven Men*, "A Case for Langdale Pike" mixes together fictional and historical figures and events. For instance, Catherine Walters was the real name of Skittles, the most celebrated courtesan of her time. Frederick, Lord Ickenham is better known to P. G. Wodehouse fans as the inventively mischievous Uncle Fred. Decadent poet Enoch Soames appears in a famous Beerbohm story (but is it just a story?). Karswell, the necromancer in M. R. James's chilling "Casting the Runes," is undone by his own evil power. Miskatonic University features in H. P. Lovecraft's horror mythos; its library possesses a rare copy of the dreaded *Necronomicon* of the mad Arab Abdul Alhazred. Lambert Strether and Little Bilham famously talk about life in Henry James's *The Ambassadors*. Harry Flashman is, of

course, the notorious rake and poltroon chronicled by George MacDonald Fraser. Needless to
say, these are just some of the tongue-in-cheek
jokes and perhaps overly recondite allusions that
make up "A Case for Langdale Pike."

"A Series of Tales"

Vincent Starrett once observed that Conan
Doyle "wrote scores of novels and short stories
as entertaining as any in the saga of Sherlock
Holmes" and "it is well to have the fact restated
at intervals for the benefit of the young." Starrett then went on to point to the Professor Challenger adventures, the supernatural tales, and the
Brigadier Gerard stories. These are obviously the
principal works—of fiction, at least—to read after one has absorbed the irreplaceable canon itself. But what other Conan Doyle books deserve
rediscovery?

First of all, there are Conan Doyle's historical
romances, the novels he long thought his best:
The White Company (1891) and its later prequel
Sir Nigel (1906). I was never drawn to either as
a boy, because knights somehow struck me as
hokey. Too much clanking armor, perhaps. More

recently, general opinion seems to dismiss the pair as "a snore," largely because Conan Doyle overburdened them with his research. As Hugh Kingsmill long ago observed of *The White Company*, "None of the persons in the book can stir a step without bumping into material out of Conan Doyle's notebooks." As a result, the two linked novels—both revolve around Sir Nigel Loring—are generally regarded as little more than faded medieval tapestries, and just about as exciting. But I wonder if people have actually opened *The White Company* recently.

In my view, it is far more than "a correct picture of the age"—as its author once called the novel—and far more entertaining than its sorry reputation would lead one to believe. Yes, the vocabulary and syntax can seem quaintly archaic at times, but Conan Doyle nonetheless injects a wonderful bounce and sweetness into the narrative. In these pages everything is springlike, full of the sap and exuberance of youth. It's also quietly funny throughout.

The plot is simple. Alleyne Edricsson has been brought up in the monastery of Beaulieu, but at the age of twenty is sent out into the world. His late father's bequest insisted that he be given what we might call a "gap year" to see life before choosing either a secular or religious vocation. Now, the realist novel has been defined—by Stendhal—as a mirror traveling down a roadway, and that virtually describes *The White Company*, especially its rumbustious initial chapters. As Alleyne trudges along toward the estate of his scoundrel brother, he encounters a Chaucerian parade of medieval folk—artists and acrobats and thieves and murderers and scholars and soldiers and peasants, and finally a damsel in distress. Eventually, Alleyne joins the esteemed and chivalric Sir Nigel Loring's company of archers, sails to France, and there begins a series of dashing adventures.

Throughout *The White Company* the reader repeatedly feels the influence of Conan Doyle's beloved Macaulay and Scott behind the rhetorical sweep and cadence of even the simplest sentences: "From sea to sea there was stringing of bows in the cottage and clang of steel in the castle." Since the author of the Sherlock Holmes stories is so adept at plain speaking, it's good to be reminded that he also commanded the high style. Alleyne finds himself falling in love with the Lady Maude: "Stronger than reason, stronger than cloister teachings, stronger than all that might hold him back, was that old, old tyrant who will brook no rival in the kingdom of youth."

Sometimes, Conan Doyle allows himself an almost Rabelaisian verbal gusto: "I have seen Frenchmen fight both in open field, in the intaking and the defending of towns or castlewicks, in escalades, camisades, night forays, bushments, sallies, outfalls, and knightly spear-runnings." At other times, he could be Tolstoy describing a young man's confusion during his first experience of battle. When Sir Nigel's ship goes into combat against two heavily armed pirate vessels, Alleyne is standing by its tiller:

> "What was that?" he asked, as a hissing, sharp-drawn voice seemed to whisper in his ear. The steersman smiled, and pointed with his foot to where a short heavy cross-bow quarrel stuck quivering in the boards. At the same instant the man stumbled forward upon his knees, and lay lifeless upon the deck, a blood-stained feather jutting out from his back. As Alleyne stooped to raise him, the air seemed to be alive with the sharp zip-zip of the bolts, and he could hear them pattering on the deck like apples at a tree-shaking.

I love that "zip-zip" and the sheer genius of "pattering on the deck like apples at a tree-shaking."

Conan Doyle is just as superb in his creation of characters. Here is the reader's first glimpse of the novel's paragon of chivalry:

> Sir Nigel was a slight man of poor stature, with a soft lisping voice and gentle ways. So short was he that his wife, who was no very tall woman, had the better of him by the breadth of three fingers. His sight having been injured in his early wars by a basketful of lime which had been emptied over him when he led the Earl of Derby's stormers up the breach at Bergerac, he had contracted something of a stoop, with a blinking, peering expression of face . . . .

As for Lady Loring,

> Her face was large and square and red, with fierce, thick brows, and the eyes of one who was accustomed to rule. Taller and broader than her husband, her flowing gown of sendal, and fur-lined tippet, could not conceal the gaunt and ungraceful outlines of her figure. It was the age of martial women . . . . Yet even in that age it was thought that, though a lady might have a soldier's heart, it was scarce as well that she should have a soldier's face. There were men who said

that of all the stern passages and daring deeds by which Sir Nigel Loring had proved the true temper of his courage, not the least was his wooing and winning of so forbidding a dame.

Needless to say, Sir Nigel absolutely adores his wife and she him.

Now, should any of Conan Doyle's readers tire of noble exploits, they can always turn for relief to the writer's several pirate stories, the best of them gathered together as *The Dealings of Captain Sharkey*. There's nothing in the least chivalric about Sharkey, as cruel and heartless an outlaw as ever hoisted the Jolly Roger. All four of the stories about him chronicle versions of the "biter bit," climaxing with sudden plot reverses and the revelation that things aren't quite as they had seemed. Nor people either.

Since these piratical exploits are set in the eighteenth century, Conan Doyle writes an appropriately elegant discursive prose. Notice how different it sounds from the medieval tone of *The White Company*:

When the great wars of the Spanish Succession had been brought to an end by the Treaty of Utrecht, the vast number of privateers which had been fitted out by the contending parties found their occupation gone. Some took to the more peaceful but less lucrative ways of ordinary commerce, others were absorbed into the fishing-fleets, and a few of the more reckless hoisted the Jolly Roger at the mizzen and the bloody flag at the main, declaring a private war upon their own account against the whole human race.

Captain Sharkey, master of the twenty-gun pirate barque *The Happy Delivery*, is the worst of a distinctly bad lot. When he passes down a coast, he leaves it littered with "gutted vessels and murdered men." Nevertheless, we learn that among all pirates

flashes of grotesque generosity alternated with longer stretches of inconceivable ferocity, and the skipper who fell into their hands might find himself dismissed with his cargo, after serving as boon companion in some hideous debauch, or might sit at his cabin table with his own nose and his lips served with pepper and salt in front of him.

In two stories old Sharkey brilliantly fools the authorities; in another a beautiful young girl becomes his prisoner, much to his eventual regret, and in the final tale, one of Sharkey's victims bides patiently for years until he is able to avenge the murder of his wife and sons.

In 1922 Conan Doyle gathered together the preponderance of his miscellaneous short fiction in six small volumes: *Tales of the Ring and Camp, Tales of Pirates and Blue Water, Tales of Terror and Mystery, Tales of Twilight and the Unseen, Tales of Adventure and Medical Life,* and *Tales of Long Ago.* In one of the great book bargains of our time, all 76 stories from these individual collections can be found together in a thick, cheap, and well-printed omnibus, available from several publishers, called *The Conan Doyle Stories.*

That brick of a book includes, for instance, "A Straggler of '15," an account of the last days of Gregory Brewster, an old soldier who decades earlier had won renown at Waterloo. A genuine tearjerker, the story came to the attention of none other than Bram Stoker, the author of *Dracula.* Stoker, as the longtime stage manager for the actor Sir Henry Irving, bought the rights for his boss, who turned it into a one-act melodrama called *Waterloo*. It came to rank among Irving's greatest theatrical triumphs.

Tales of the Ring reminds us that Conan Doyle was always an ardent sportsman. As a boy, he captained a scrappy gang of Catholic youths in Edinburgh and was notably good with his fists. Even the often sedentary Sherlock Holmes is a superb pugilist, once querying a former champion in *The Sign of the Four:* "I don't think you can have forgotten me. Don't you remember the amateur who fought three rounds with you at Alison's rooms on the night of your benefit four years back?" Conan Doyle himself was actually invited to referee the 1910 world championship heavyweight bout between Jim Jeffries and the African American Jack Johnson. With real regret, he was forced to decline, in part because he couldn't easily travel to Reno, Nevada.

Of the *Tales of the Ring and Camp*, the standout is "The Croxley Master," a vivid insider's account of a boxing championship in a coalmining district during the 1880s. A young medical student, desperate for cash to pay his tuition, bravely goes up against the reigning champ, widely known as "the Master." Halfway through the story, Conan Doyle pauses to explain the appeal of blood sports to these miners:

Literature, art, science, all these things were beyond their horizon; but the race, the football match, the cricket, the fight, these were things which they could understand, which they could speculate upon in advance and comment upon afterwards. Sometimes brutal, sometimes grotesque, the love of sport is still one of the great agencies which make for the happiness of our people. It lies very deeply in the springs of our nature, and when it has been educated out, a higher, more refined nature may be left, but it will not be of that robust British type which has left its mark so deeply on the world.

Conan Doyle himself chose *Tales of Long Ago* as the single group of stories he would most want to preserve. In "The Last of the Legions," the Roman troops are withdrawn from England, leaving the country in the hands of the native Britons, who have long lobbied for self-rule. "Be careful what you wish for" is one lesson from its denouement. More subtly, it implicitly justifies wise colonial governance. Similarly, "The Last Galley" juxtaposes Carthaginian softness and decadence with Roman virtue and manliness. In it, a seer predicts that Rome herself will eventually grow sybaritic and weak, then collapse—and be replaced by England. Will the British Empire continue the same pattern of decline and fall? Conan Doyle tells us that when the surviving citizens of Carthage looked down on the ruins of their former capital, "they understood that it is the law of heaven that the world is given to the hard and to the self-denying, whilst he who would escape the duties of manhood will soon be stripped of the pride, the wealth, and the power, which are the prizes which manhood brings." England, take heed!

For all its capaciousness, even this mighty omnibus fails to include all the short work by Conan Doyle still worth reading. The title story of the volume *Danger! and Other Stories*—first published in July 1914 before the outbreak of World War I—warns the Edwardian military about the devastating effects of submarine attacks. Captain Sirius and his fleet blow up all the ships transporting food to England and thus bring the mighty island nation to its knees. Related in the form of the captain's logbook, and packed with technical details, this cautionary tale possesses an almost documentary realism. According to Conan Doyle's bibliographers, *Danger!* was particularly well received in Germany—so much so that "the German Secretary of the Navy bestowed warm praise" upon its author "in the Reichstag on 1 May 1917." Conan Doyle found this a rather uncomfortable compliment.

Most of these stories are easy enough to locate, but I want to recommend, with only minor reservations, four of Conan Doyle's harder-to-find novels about contemporary life: *Beyond the City* (1893), *The Stark Munro Letters* (1894), *A Duet with an Occasional Chorus* (1899), and *The Tragedy of the "Korosko"* (1898). All are entertaining (and often quite funny), yet too seldom read today. For the most part, they are based on periods or episodes in Conan Doyle's own life.

In *Beyond the City* three families take up residence in the new London suburbs. Among them is the marvelously ebullient, shrewd, and shockingly emancipated Mrs. Westmacott. Two spinsters pay her a social call, and she asks if they would like some stout:

> "I am sorry that I have no tea to offer you. I look upon the subserviency of woman as largely due to her abandoning nutritious drinks and invigorating exercises to the male. I do neither." She picked up a pair of fifteen-pound dumb-bells from beside the fireplace

and swung them lightly about her head. "You see what may be done on stout," said she.

When the elder Miss Williams protests that "woman has a mission of her own," Mrs. Westmacott drops her dumbbells with a crash:

> "The old cant!" she cried. "The old shibboleth! What is this mission which is reserved for woman? All that is humble, that is mean, that is soul-killing, that is so contemptible and so ill-paid that none other will touch it. All that is woman's mission. And who imposed those limitations upon her? Who cooped her up within this narrow sphere? Was it Providence? Was it nature? No, it was the arch-enemy. It was man."

In the course of the novel, two young sisters fall in love, financial crises threaten to ruin the lives of everyone, and, at the climax, the *dea ex machina* is, of course, the indomitable Mrs. Westmacott. While the plotting of *Beyond the City* is fairly perfunctory, the charm of the book lies in its pervasive humor, brisk narration, and lightness of touch. In my favorite chapters the two sisters, hoping to thwart a suspected romance between their father and Mrs. Westmacott, take the precepts of female emancipation beyond the limits and, in company with their hapless fiancés, create a shocking tableau of Saturnalian license. Their poor father returns home to find his living room filled with blue smoke, strewn with oyster shells and empty champagne bottles, and his beautiful daughters smoking cigarettes and lounging on settees in the most indecorous postures. It's all quite delightful.

Once during an interview, Conan Doyle summed up his first days as a doctor:

> I settled in practice, first in Plymouth and then, after a few months, at Southsea, the fashionable suburb of Portsmouth. My adventures in that rather romantic period, and all my mental and spiritual aspirations, are written down in *The Stark Munro Letters*, a book which, with the exception of one chapter, is a very close autobiography.

Much of this novel—composed of a series of letters by John Stark Munro to an American friend—concentrates on the protagonist's religious doubts, his eagerness to come to some kind of understanding of God and life's purpose, and the typical hormonal confusions of a young man. Among them are "shrinking, horrible shyness, alternating with occasional absurd fits of audacity which represent the reaction against it, the longing for close friendship, the agonies over imaginary slights, the extraordinary sexual doubts, the deadly fears caused by non-existent diseases, the vague emotion produced by all women, and the half-frightened thrill by particular ones, the aggressiveness caused by fear of being afraid, the suddenly blacknesses, the profound self-distrust. . . ."

Talky and earnest at times, *The Stark Munro Letters* might be called Conan Doyle's *Portrait of the Artist as a Young Man*. What carries the reader along, however, is its depiction of the charismatic Cullingworth, a con man of W. C. Fields–like self-confidence and ebullience. Once a fellow medical student with Stark Munro, the go-getting Cullingworth—based on a Dr. George Turnavine Budd—resides in a thirty-bedroom mansion, though only the hall and dining room are properly furnished. The fast-talking doctor offers free medical advice, which brings in patients by the hundreds, then makes all his money on the medicines he prescribes and which his wife makes up. He's also a part-time inventor, developing a super-magnet that will deflect cannonballs from warships. In many ways, he's a more raffish cousin to Mrs. Westmacott and Professor Challenger. Cullingworth regularly calls Stark Munro "Laddie," shamelessly reads other people's mail, argues that doctors should lobby against the improvement of sanitation, since it would cut down on their business, smashes windows when they're stuck shut, and even orders his bewildered partner to begin writing a novel:

"But I never wrote a line in my life."

"A properly balanced man can do anything he sets his hand to. He's got every possible quality inside him, and all he wants is the will to develop it."

"Could you write a novel yourself?" I asked

"Of course I could. Such a novel, Munro, that when they'd read the first chapter the folk would just sit groaning until the second came out. They'd wait in rows outside my door in the hope of hearing what was coming next. By Crums, I'll go and begin it now!" And, with another somersault over the end of the bed, he rushed from the room, with the tassels of his dressing gown flying behind him.

Stark Munro eventually settles down to his own practice, survives a crisis or two, and happily marries. As for Cullingworth, when last seen this "Napoleon of medicine" is on the run from creditors and heading for South America.

A Duet with an Occasional Chorus is Conan Doyle's most domestic novel, both winsome and witty. In it he traces the courtship and early married life of a young couple named Maude and Frank Crosse. What could sound more dull? Yet the book earned the admiration of H. G. Wells and is a favorite among many Doyleans. Though a bit corny at the beginning, the writing is generally sprightly, with a good deal of bantering conversation. It would make an excellent play.

One evening, for instance, Maude compels Frank to admit that he had cared for other women before he met her. How many precisely? Frank confesses to having been almost continuously infatuated with one woman or another since adolescence. Oh, really! Maude then discloses that she too has had "experiences." Once she was left alone with a gentleman who had come to visit her mother. In short order, he had kissed her and she had kissed him back, and then he had asked her to sit upon his knee. "Yek!" exclaims Frank, appalled and sickened. Why didn't she scream?

Or leave the room? Well, answers Maude, the dark gentleman was holding her and "there was another reason." Which was? "Well, I wasn't very good at walking at that time," she explains. "You see, I was only three years old." Frank is suitably abashed.

Early on the couple draw up a set of "Maxims for the Married"—number 1 is "Since you are married, you may as well make the best of it," and number 13 is "There is only one thing worse than quarrels in public. That is caresses." In other chapters Frank discusses his favorite writers, Maude and some friends try to start a book club (and end up gossiping instead), and, eventually, a serious financial crisis nearly leads the couple to bankruptcy. But all these pale before the most serious threat to the marriage. One morning Frank receives a letter from his former mistress, insisting that they meet secretly at their old restaurant. Violet, it turns out, wants to restart the affair, and when Frank protests, she dryly tells him, "You speak as if a man ceased to live because he is married."

When this chapter appeared, it shocked contemporary readers. But as Conan Doyle said, "I did not set out to write a fairy tale, but to draw a living couple with all the weaknesses, temptations, and sorrows which might come to test their characters and to overshadow their lives." Oddly enough, even though the book evokes what is thought to be Conan Doyle's early married life with Touie, he presented the original manuscript to Jean Leckie. Touie was still alive and he and Jean were not to marry until 1907.

Of all Conan Doyle's realist novels about the contemporary world, the most popular during his lifetime was *The Tragedy of the "Korosko."* A boatload of tourists, traveling up the Nile, is captured by a band of Islamic fundamentalists, loyal to the memory of the Mahdi, the Osama bin Laden of his time. Over the course of the next two days some of the westerners will die violently and all will be severely tested. The kidnapped—among them, an Irish Catholic couple, a middle-aged English solicitor, a retired British soldier, a volatile Frenchman, and a young American graduate of Smith College and her elderly aunt—will eventually be offered a choice: If they agree to accept Islam, they will be permitted to live. Otherwise, the men will be killed and the women. . . .

Conan Doyle skillfully builds up the suspense. Rescuers may or may not be coming. One of the prisoners has managed to secrete a small pistol—with three bullets in it, just enough to save the women from a fate worse than death. Stalling for time, the captives ask for a mullah to instruct them in the fundamentals of Islam. He turns out to be a kindly and scholarly old man who calls them "my lambs." Should the prisoners accept or at least pretend to accept the ways of Allah just to save their lives? Can they bow to Mecca? Will they or won't they renounce Christianity? Then suddenly, before they know it, their time is up and the moment of decision arrives.

"Good Night, Mister Sherlock Holmes"

⊠ Long ago, Ward, Lock & Co., in a publishing circular, announced *A Study in Scarlet* as the lead feature in the 1887 *Beeton's* Christmas Annual:

> This story will be found remarkable for the
> skillful presentation of a supremely ingenious
> detective, whose performances, while based
> on the most rational principles, outshine any
> hitherto depicted. . . . The surprises are most
> cleverly and yet most naturally managed, and
> at each stage the reader's attention is kept
> fascinated and eager for the next event . . . .
> It is certain to be read, not once, but twice by
> every reader, and the person who can take

it up and lay it down again unfinished must be one of those rare people who are neither impressionable nor curious. *A Study in Scarlet* should be the talk of every Christmas gathering throughout the land.

Despite all this intelligent enthusiasm, *Beeton's* clearly had no idea that it was introducing one of the greatest characters in world literature. Sherlock Holmes was, in fact, no mere detective; he was The Great Detective, the profession's Platonic ideal, a legend not only in his own time but ever since. As Arthur Conan Doyle's brother-in-law famously punned, "Though he might be more humble, there's no police like Holmes."

Eccentric aesthete, amateur boxer, and baritsu adept, master of disguise, expert chemist and linguist, occasional philosopher and overall polymath, an entrepreneur who lives by his wits, the Sleuth of Baker Street is all that and more. Hesketh Pearson once said that Sherlock Holmes is "what every man desires to be," nothing less than "the knight-errant who rescues the unfortunate and fights single-handed against the powers of darkness."

But, of course, he is not single-handed. "Good old Watson!" murmurs Holmes at the end of

"The Last Bow," when, on the eve of World War I, the detective comes out of retirement to defeat the German spy Von Bork. "You are the one fixed point in a changing world." More than anything else, the Holmes saga portrays a deepening friendship and ultimately chronicles how Dr. John H. Watson gradually humanizes this great thinking machine. Among the moments of highest drama in the entire canon is that when, in "The Three Garridebs," the good doctor is shot:

> "You're not hurt, Watson! For God's sake, say that you are not hurt!'"
>
> It was worth a wound—it was worth many wounds—to know the depth of loyalty and love which lay behind that cold mask. The clear, hard eyes were dimmed for a moment, and the firm lips were shaking. For the one and only time I caught a glimpse of a great heart as well as of a great brain. All my years of humble but singled-minded service culminated in that moment of revelation.

"Any studies in Sherlock Holmes," Ronald Knox said, "must be, first and foremost, studies in Dr. Watson." Though he refers to himself as the whetstone against which Holmes sharpens his wits,

Watson is hardly the bumbling idiot portrayed by Nigel Bruce in the 1940s movies with Basil Rathbone. He is a former soldier, a man of action, easy to get on with, manly, direct, and utterly dependable. While Holmes lives entirely for his work, disdains every form of society, and resorts to dangerous drugs when bored, Watson not only pursues an active medical practice but also marries at least twice, enjoys reading for pleasure (Clark Russell's sea stories being particular favorites), likes to play an occasional game of billiards with friends, and regularly takes a flier on the horse races. He is even something of a ladies' man—"the fair sex is your department, Watson." Notwithstanding his unswerving loyalty to Holmes, this rock of common sense and decency doesn't hesitate to criticize the detective's moral judgment in callously trifling with a maid's affections, vocally disapproves of his cocaine addiction, and generally puts up with a lot of guff. "Really, Holmes," as he says wearily in *The Valley of Fear*, "you are a little trying at times."

In vaudeville, a comedy team's straight man often earned more than the comic: It took the rarest skill and timing to set up the jokes in just the right way. Just so, Watson is Holmes's straight man, the audience and butt of all those antic capers and dazzling feats of ratiocination. "I will do nothing serious without my trusted comrade and biographer at my elbow." How could he? Without Watson's case studies, we might know almost nothing of Holmes the sleuth hound, Holmes the logician, Holmes the modern wizard of Baker Street. If Conan Doyle had truly wanted to kill off the Great Detective, observed the novelist John Fowles, "the most effective way . . . would have been to kill off Watson."

Agatha Christie's Hercule Poirot once referred to "*The Adventures of Sherlock Holmes*," then reverently murmured the single word "*Maître.*" Was the little Belgian referring to Holmes?

> "Ah, non, non, not Sherlock Holmes! It is the author, Sir Arthur Conan Doyle, that I salute. These tales of Sherlock Holmes are in reality far-fetched, full of fallacies and most artificially contrived. But the art of writing—ah, that is entirely different. The pleasure of the language, the creation above all of that magnificent character, Dr. Watson. Ah, that was indeed a triumph."

Christie is just one of a series of writers who have recognized and honored the artistry of Arthur Conan Doyle. John le Carré has pointed out the

Sherlock Holmes stories' "narrative perfection," emphasizing, like Dorothy L. Sayers before him, their masterly "interplay between dialogue and description, perfect characterization and perfect timing." Peter Ackroyd has spoken of the "melancholy intensity and majestic cadence" of Conan Doyle's prose, "striated with rich local detail, so that he seems effortlessly able to evoke the marvelous and the terrible in the ordinary." Distinguished novelists as different as Eric Ambler, P. G. Wodehouse, Angus Wilson, and Graham Greene have all been proud to introduce new editions of the tales of Baker Street.

Even in this metafictional age, Conan Doyle's narrative artistry can stand up to the most intensive analysis; indeed it almost prefigures aspects of hypertext: "Nearly all the Holmes stories," recently wrote novelist Michael Chabon, "are stories of people who tell their stories, and every so often the stories these people tell feature people telling stories." Thus a client relates a crime or strange incident, after which Watson chronicles the course of the investigation. But this is just the beginning. "The investigation in turn produces the story of how the crime was committed, or of the genuine meaning behind the seemingly inexplicable occurrence." Finally, once the malefactor is caught, he or she "may introduce an entirely new version of the story, by way of pointing out certain flaws in Holmes's reasoning or confirming his wildest surmises, and then offering reasons for the crime, reasons that can have their roots in yet another story, often one that played out many years before. And then we are back in Baker Street, to be handed over by Watson to the next story."

All that Chabon says is true, and yet one might still prefer Vincent Starrett's even more fundamental critical insight: "I like the kind of fiction in which things happen, and then keep on happening."

When all is said and done, despite the underappreciated Dr. Watson to whom we owe so much and despite Conan Doyle's obvious storytelling gifts, it is only Holmes who truly makes our hearts beat faster. As the popular Jeremy Brett television series, the steampunk *Sherlock Holmes* of Robert Downey Jr., and the BBC's twenty-first-century text-messaging *Sherlock* have shown, Holmes remains a great marketing commodity and a timeless archetype, adaptable to any era and format. Happily, the three series also present attractive and admirable Watsons.

But ultimately Sherlock steals any show he's in: His trademark deerstalker, Inverness cape, calabash pipe, and magnifying glass have made him iconographically recognizable the world over. From the very beginning the celebrated criminologist was more than just a creature made of words on a page. A volume like Bill Blackbeard's *Sherlock Holmes in America* gathers together hundreds of images of the detective in magazines, comics, advertisements, and popular culture. It reminds us that we don't merely hear and read of Sherlock everywhere, we see him too.

Sidney Paget's original period illustrations for the *Strand Magazine* carry canonical authenticity, and some of his images—of Holmes and Watson traveling by train or of the struggle at the Reichenbach Falls—do linger in the memory. But many Baker Street aficionados prefer Frederic Dorr Steele's depiction of a far better looking detective. Between 1903 and 1905 Steele drew 46 illustrations for the *Collier's Weekly* appearances of *The Return of Sherlock Holmes*, most notably ten full-color portraits for the cover. Many of these Steele images, whether framed originals or thumbtacked facsimiles, hang on the walls in the homes of Baker Street Irregulars.

Steele based his rendering of the detective on the actor William Gillette, who originated the title role in the stage play *Sherlock Holmes* and starred in it for forty years. In a letter to the actor, the writer Booth Tarkington spoke for a generation when he said, "I would rather see you play Sherlock Holmes than be a child again on Christmas morning." On the silver screen Holmes has been vividly portrayed in series starring Eille Norwood, Arthur Wontner, and, above all, Basil Rathbone, just to name three. But then more films have been made about Sherlock Holmes than any other fictional character.

Yet few of the full-length, post-Rathbone movies about the detective have ever been entirely successful. In *The Seven-Per-Cent Solution*—a rather kinky film shot as if it were a lighthearted Viennese operetta—Holmes undergoes both cocaine withdrawal and treatment with Dr. Sigmund Freud. The fast-moving and Indiana Jones–like *Young Sherlock Holmes* suffers from a surprisingly downbeat ending. Some of the more unusual big-screen exploits include *The Adventures of Sherlock Holmes's Smarter Brother*, the bizarre Sherlockian fantasy *They Might be Giants*, and Billy Wilder's *Private Life of Sherlock Holmes* (revealing the secret of the Loch Ness monster).

All have their moments, without being fully satisfying. Two of the most admired of the more modern films, *A Study in Terror* and *Murder by Decree*, pit Holmes against Jack the Ripper. In the end I still think Sherlock Holmes figures at his movie-palace best in Rathbone's atmospheric *Hound of the Baskervilles* and *Adventures of Sherlock Holmes*, the latter brilliantly shot, with touches of almost Expressionist camera work.

Over the years I've acquired tapes or DVDs of all these and other Sherlock Holmes movies, as well as audiobooks of the stories and cassettes of the sometimes kitschy, but still atmospheric radio shows of the 1940s. My shelves include perhaps a hundred works by or about Conan Doyle. But ultimately mine is simply an enthusiastic reader's library—various editions of the novels and stories, the major biographies and reference works. Nothing really exceptional.

By contrast, some of my fellow Irregulars possess truly eye-popping collections. One friend has gathered hundreds of editions of *The Hound of the Baskervilles*, another owns, along with much else, T. S. Eliot's copy of *The Complete Sherlock Holmes Short Stories*, and still another can show you the holograph of Conan Doyle's *A Duet with an Occasional Chorus*. Irregulars have acquired everything from Conan Doyle's desk blotter to a thumb-sized chip of wood from one of his bookshelves. One of the most devoted disciples of the Master owns sixty-two Sherlockian Christmas ornaments, each slyly, often punningly, representing one of the sixty canonical stories. Those extra two ornaments are little jokes: A fish made out of crimson felt is—wait for it—a red herring, while a pinecone stuck to a small can of oil forms a rebus for the author, Cone and Oil.

Does all this seem silly? I don't think so. Collecting, starting clubs, holding annual dinners and conferences, writing essays and pastiches— all these are expressions of love. And not just for those old-timey stories about two guys solving crimes in late Victorian England. Because of The Baker Street Irregulars, my friends now include a retired judge, a professional screen actor, a distinguished cardiac surgeon, the chief toxicologist of New York City, the owner of a Manhattan bookstore, the head of a university anthropology department, the former chief technical officer for Apple, an eminent rare book librarian, a longtime Pentagon strategist, several novelists and journalists, lots of lawyers, and the proprietors of two of my favorite small presses. If I'm ever in trouble, all I have to do is call on The Baker Street Irregulars.

This little book is subtitled *The Whole Art of Storytelling*, and I hope it has shown that A. Conan Doyle was much more than just the literary agent for those denizens of 221B Baker Street. Whether you're looking for mystery or horror, science fiction or romance, social realism or historical fiction, memoir or essay, Arthur Conan Doyle is the writer for you.

For good or ill, he's also a writer to turn to if you're seriously interested in Spiritualism. From 1916 to 1930 Conan Doyle published thirteen books about the subject, but I've only read most of two: *The History of Spiritualism* and *The Edge of the Unknown*. I found both lively and enjoyable as period entertainments. There are accounts of famous mediums—the Fox Sisters, D. D. Home—and re-creations of séances, encounters with the skeptical Houdini, conversations with famous dead writers, and much else to amuse the cynical. I haven't the heart to open *The Coming of the Fairies,* in which the creator of Sherlock Holmes argues for the possible existence of little winged people.

To be fair, a preoccupation with fairies ran in the Conan Doyle family. Most notably, Uncle Dicky—Victorian artist Richard Doyle—created many beloved illustrations for books about Fairyland. Anyone who reads a lot of Conan Doyle also comes to recognize that this lapsed Catholic pondered the mysteries of time and space, of being and nothingness, throughout his life. As a young man he joined the Society for Psychical Research. In his fiction the spiritual—in the largest sense—is a recurrent theme: Indian mysticism in his first novel *The Mystery of Cloomber*, the supernatural throughout his "twilight tales," the search for belief by young Stark Munro, the conflict between Islam and Christianity in *The Tragedy of the "Korosko."* Still, as Conan Doyle once wrote,

> I might have drifted on for my whole life as a psychical researcher, showing a sympathetic, but more or less dilettante attitude towards the whole subject, as if we were arguing about some impersonal thing such as the existence of Atlantis or the Baconian controversy. But the War came, and when the War came it brought earnestness into all our souls and made us look more closely at our own beliefs and reassess their values.

While Conan Doyle may have been naïve or gullible about Spiritualism, I admire his willingness to follow through on his beliefs, even when the whole world mocked them and him. That said, few of us are ever likely to read *Pheneas Speaks*. As T. S. Eliot once said, "Sir Arthur Conan Doyle, the eminent spiritualist . . . what has he to do with Sherlock Holmes?"

For we do come back to Baker Street in the end, to 1890s London, to threatening Dartmoor, to a certain dark night at Pondicherry Lodge, to a bucolic countryside that sometimes rivals in sin "the lowest and vilest alleys" of the metropolis. Does anyone ever forget the insidious threat found in five orange pips, or the dog that did nothing in the night-time, or the cipher of "the dancing men," or the hideous death inflicted by "the devil's foot"? Who doesn't shiver at the mere mention of "the band, the speckled band!" or shudder at the memory of the insidious Professor Moriarty, or yearn to know more of Mycroft Holmes, who sometimes "is the British government"?

As long as readers exist, young people will be discovering Sherlock Holmes and thrilling to the immortal promise: "Come Watson, come, the game is afoot!" As Vincent Starrett long ago declared, these two will always live "in a romantic chamber of the heart, in a nostalgic country of the mind, where it is always 1895."

But what shall I read next? Perhaps having loved *The White Company*, I should go on to some of Conan Doyle's other historical novels, such as *The Great Shadow* (1892) and *Rodney Stone* (1896). Or maybe I should try his last, reportedly very muddled book, *The Maracot Deep* (1929), in which a Challenger-like team discovers Atlantis, and Atlanteans, on the bottom of the sea. One of these days, I'll surely get to all these. But just now I feel it's time to reread *The Hound of the Baskervilles*. It's a dark and chilly night, and there's nobody at home. First, I'll just turn off a few of these lights. Now where is that bottle of Orange Crush? In my beginning is my end.

▣ APPENDIX

"Education Never Ends, Watson"

Essential Books by Arthur Conan Doyle

The Complete Sherlock Holmes (numerous editions:
The Oxford Sherlock Holmes, The Annotated Sherlock Holmes, and *The New Annotated Sherlock Holmes* are outstanding in their differing ways)

The Captain of the Polestar: Weird and Imaginative Fiction by Arthur Conan Doyle, edited by Christopher Roden and Barbara Roden

The Conan Doyle Stories

The Exploits of Brigadier Gerard and *The Adventures of Gerard*

The Lost World

The Poison Belt

The White Company

Essential Books about Arthur Conan Doyle

A. Conan Doyle, *Memories and Adventures*
A. Conan Doyle, *Through the Magic Door*
Arthur Conan Doyle: A Life in Letters, edited by Jon
    Lellenberg, Daniel Stashower, and Charles Foley
John Dickson Carr, *The Life of Sir Arthur Conan
    Doyle*
Owen Dudley Edwards, *In Quest of Sherlock Holmes*
Roger Lancelyn Green and John Michael Gibson, *A
    Bibliography of A. Conan Doyle*
Jon Lellenberg, *The Quest for Sir Arthur Conan Doyle*
Andrew Lycett, *The Man Who Created Sherlock Holmes*
Daniel Stashower, *Teller of Tales: The Life of Arthur
    Conan Doyle*

Essential Books about Sherlock Holmes

W. S. Baring-Gould, *The Annotated Sherlock Holmes*
Bill Blackbeard, *Sherlock Holmes in America*
D. Martin Dakin, *A Sherlock Holmes Commentary*
Steven Doyle and David A. Crowder, *Sherlock Holmes
    for Dummies*
Michael Harrison, *In the Footsteps of Sherlock Holmes*
Leslie S. Klinger, *The New Annotated Sherlock Holmes*
Leslie S. Klinger and Laurie R. King, *The Grand Game*
Christopher Morley, *The Standard Doyle Company:
    Christopher Morley on Sherlock Holmes,* edited by
    Steven Rothman
Christopher Redmond, *A Sherlock Holmes Handbook*
Barbara and Christopher Roden, eds., *The Case-Files
    of Sherlock Holmes* (individual volumes of essay
    and commentary on "The Musgrave Ritual," "The

Speckled Band," "The Blue Carbuncle," and "The Dying Detective")

Edgar W. Smith, *Profile by Gaslight: An Irregular Reader about the Private Life of Sherlock Holmes*

Vincent Starrett, *The Private Life of Sherlock Holmes*

Vincent Starrett, *Sherlock Alive,* edited by Karen Murdock

Jack Tracy, *The Encyclopedia Sherlockiana*

Some Classic Works Featuring Sherlock Holmes

Adrian Conan Doyle and John Dickson Carr, *The Exploits of Sherlock Holmes*

Michael Dibdin, *The Last Sherlock Holmes Story*

August Derleth, *The Adventures of Solar Pons* and its sequels (Pons is essentially Holmes under another name)

Loren D. Estleman, *Sherlock Holmes vs. Dracula*

John Gardner, *The Revenge of Moriarty*

Nicholas Meyer, *The Seven-Per-Cent Solution*

Manly Wade Wellman and Wade Wellman, *Sherlock Holmes's War of the Worlds*

Some Twenty-First-Century Works of Fiction Inspired by Sherlock Holmes, A. Conan Doyle, or The Baker Street Irregulars

John Joseph Adams, ed., *The Improbable Adventures of Sherlock Holmes* (includes Neil Gaiman's "A Study in Emerald" and Barbara Roden's "The Things That Shall Come upon Them")

Julian Barnes, *Arthur & George*

Caleb Carr, *The Italian Secretary*

Michael Chabon, *The Final Solution*

Lyndsay Faye, *Dust and Shadow*

Martin Greenberg, Jon L. Lellenberg, and Daniel Stashower, eds., *Sherlock Holmes in America* (includes, among other stories and essays, Lloyd Rose's "Ghost in the Machine")

Mark Haddon, *The Curious Incident of the Dog in the Night-Time*

Steve Hockensmith, *Holmes on the Range*

Anthony Horowitz, *The House of Silk*

Laurie R. King, *The Art of Detection*

Jon Lellenberg, *Baker Street Irregular* (featuring many well-known BSI members in a story of social change and espionage)

Graham Moore, *The Sherlockian*

Online

There are many websites devoted to Sherlock Holmes and Arthur Conan Doyle. I recommend visits to *The Baker Street Journal* (bakerstreetjournal.com), The Baker Street Blog (bakerstreetblog.com), The Best of Sherlock Holmes (bestofsherlock.com), The Hounds of the Internet (http://www.sherlockian.net/hounds/), The Arthur Conan Doyle Collection of the Toronto Public Library (http://www.torontopubliclibrary.ca/books-video-music/specialized-collections/literature-genre-doyle.jsp), The Sherlock Holmes Collection at the University of Minnesota (http://special.lib.umn.edu/rare/holmes.phtml), The Arthur Conan Doyle Society (http://www.ash-tree.bc.ca/acdsocy.html), and The Sherlock Holmes Society of London (http://www.sherlock-holmes.org.uk/).

▧ ACKNOWLEDGMENTS

I would like to thank Hanne Winarsky, Christopher Chung, Debbie Tegarden, Kelly Malloy, Sarah Caldwell, Julie Haenisch, Bob Bettendorf, Alison Anuzis, Jessica Pellien, Shaquona Crews, Brigitta van Rheinberg, and Tracy Baldwin at Princeton University Press. An especially grateful thank you goes to my copy editor, Jodi Beder.

Rachel Shea, Ron Charles, and my other colleagues at the *Washington Post Book World* generously allowed me a break from my weekly reviews, so that I might focus on this project. Andy Solberg deserves a special shout-out for the use of his beach house for some uninterrupted time to work on these pages. My friend Tom Mann at the Library of Congress provided some essential reference material. Peter Blau, the greatest all-round Sherlockian collector of our time, kindly lent me some books from his library.

Christopher and Barbara Roden read an initial draft of the manuscript, saved me from error, and offered invaluable advice. Dan Stashower did the same for the final proofs. Much of what I know about Conan Doyle and Sherlock Holmes I owe to them and to the work of Owen Dudley Edwards, Jon Lellenberg, Leslie Klinger, Steven Rothman, Steve Doyle, and the late Richard Lancelyn Green. Many others, through their conversation or example, contributed to my Sherlockian education, including Don Pollock, Albert, Julia, and Betsy Rosenblatt, Otto Penzler, Richard Sveum, Julie McKuras, Cliff Goldfarb, Lloyd Rose, Michael Whelan and Mary Ann Bradley, Andy Solberg (again), Susan Rice, Evelyn Herzog, Dana Richards, Thomas Cynkin, Ralph Earle, Susan Dahlinger, John Baesch, Leroy Lad Panek, Christopher Frayling, Andy Fusco, Barbara Rusch, Neil Gaiman, Scott Monty, Laurie King, Bill Vande Water, Bill Dorn, Nicholas Utechin, George A. Vanderburgh, Hartley Nathan, Catherine Cooke, Tim Johnson, Peggy Perdue, David Stuart Davies and Kathryn White, Jonathan and Elaine McCafferty, Roger Johnson, Roy Pilot, and Randall Stock. I hope that those friends I have inadvertently overlooked will for-give me. I can hardly stress enough that I alone am responsible for any mistakes or misjudg-ments in *On Conan Doyle*.

As always, my agents Glen Hartley and Lynn Chu offered their wise counsel and guidance. Not least, I want to thank Marian Peck Dirda and our sons Chris, Mike, and Nate, as well as my fellow members of the two most exclusive and shadowy groups in Washington: the Half-Pay Club and the League of Extraordinary Gentlemen.

⊞ Note: Bits and pieces of this book appeared, usually in wildly different form, in various ven-ues. Allow me to thank the *Washington Post Book World*, the Friends of the Arthur Conan Doyle Collection of the Toronto Public Library, Cana-dian Holmes, the *Baker Street Journal*, the online Barnes & Noble Review, Ash-Tree Press, and Calabash Press.

▣ BIOGRAPHICAL NOTE

Michael Dirda is a Pulitzer Prize–winning literary journalist and a longtime book columnist
for the *Washington Post*. He is the author of the
memoir *An Open Book* and of four collections
of essays: *Readings, Bound to Please, Book by
Book,* and *Classics for Pleasure.* Since 2002 he
has been an invested member of the Baker Street
Irregulars.